GOD AND DECISION-MAKING

God and decision-making

A QUAKER APPROACH

Jane Mace

First published by Quaker Books in November 2012

Quaker Books, Friends House, 173 Euston Road, London NW1 2BJ
www.quaker.org.uk

The moral rights of the author are asserted in accordance with
the Copyright, Designs and Patents Act 1988. All rights reserved.
No part of this book may be reproduced or utilised, in any form
or by any means, electronic or mechanical, without permission in
writing from the publisher. Reviewers may quote brief passages.

Enquiries should be addressed to the Publications Manager,
Quaker Books, Friends House, 173 Euston Road, London NW1 2BJ.

ISBN 978-1-907123-32-0

© Jane Mace 2012

Cover design by Quaker Communication & Services

Book designed and typeset by Cox Design, Witney

Printed by Berforts Information Press

Extracts from "The task of the recording clerk: spiritual exercise and
ministry" in *Friends Journal* © 2011 Friends Publishing Corporation.
Reprinted with permission. To subscribe: www.friendsjournal.org

While every effort has been made to contact copyright holders
of material reproduced in this book, the publisher would be
glad to rectify in future editions any errors or omissions.

CONTENTS

Introduction   VII

1. Worship, God and time   15

2. Discipline and upholding   39

3. Unity and discernment   61

4. Clerks and clerking   83

5. Reading and writing   101

6. Learning   125

Appendices   139
   Yearly Meeting Gathering 2011, minute 23
   Meeting for Sufferings April 2011, minute on BDS

Bibliography   142

INTRODUCTION

To the reader

You may be a seasoned Quaker, with many years of thinking about the subjects of this book; or you may be someone who has never been near a Quaker meeting, but is simply curious to know about ways to deal with decision-making in your own context. Between the two of you, there will, I hope, be a spectrum of other readers. For that reason, I have taken nothing for granted about Quaker language and customs. That means some of you will want to skip passages of explanation. I hope it also means you who are a visitor can join in the discussion on an equal footing. In order to strengthen that feeling, I decided to write about Quakers as "they" rather than "we", despite being a convinced Quaker myself.

The subject of this book is an approach to group decision-making that assumes a commitment to divine guidance. Although I do not know any other organisations that take this approach to carrying out their affairs, I suspect there are likely to be some: hence, the subtitle "a" rather than "the" Quaker approach.

The research

As in any religion, there are varieties of Quakers. The Quakers I know about are the ones discussed in this book: the "liberal" or "unprogrammed" variety, whose faith (theology) and practice (liturgy) are grounded in the practice of silent worship and unplanned ministry. If you are not familiar with shades of Quakerism you may be a little puzzled by that. It's a matter of emphasis. Quakers generally share a common idea of having direct access to God. But "programmed" Quakers favour a form of worship that has more in common with a church Christianity – with a pastor, hymns and prayers. Today, this form of Quaker worship is far more common than the liberal variety, which makes up less than ten per cent of world membership (Dandelion 2008, p. 113).

So the focus of my study has been on a very small sector of this international community, and more particularly on the role of clerks and their part in writing the minutes of Quaker business meetings. The business meetings that I studied are those of local and area

Quaker meetings, together with sessions of Yearly Meeting and of Meeting for Sufferings. I am aware there are a great number of other Quaker groups and committees in which a similar, worshipful approach to decision-making takes place; there is scope for further research there.

Before I began this study, some of my own experience of clerking had been difficult. That difficulty helped me form questions – always a key stage in research. At times I have felt like an anthropologist, at others like a tourist. But mostly I have felt like a reporter, asking questions and listening – not once, but over and over again – to the answers. My research background encouraged me to recognise the value of this attentiveness. In technical terms, the approach I have taken has been an "ethnographic" one, in which the work is above all to describe and then to allow themes to emerge from the descriptions.

Between January and October 2011, I undertook visits, questionnaires and interviews among Quakers in England, Scotland and Wales to discover something of current experience. Reading published guidance and thinking by Quakers on divinity and decision-making filled out the picture. The study as a whole is confined to current practice in the UK: in the spirit of open inquiry, my aim has been to bring together as many voices and experiences as possible, while accepting that any historical approach based on scholarly research into past Quaker activity was beyond the scope of the time I could give it.

As time passed and the research developed, the questions I was exploring became broader and, in a sense, deeper. I realised I could not look at either clerking or writing minutes without also looking at the experience of everybody present in the business meeting, and I began to explore further the experience not just of those at the clerks' table, but of all those in the room at a meeting for worship for business. In such meetings, as Quakers are taught, the purpose is to seek divine guidance. Knowing this, I realised that I needed to explore what this might mean – and also that this was where this book should start.

My interest

It was not a conscious search for a religious faith that drew me to

Introduction

Quaker life in early 2001, but another research project that had grown out of the issues I had been working on as an adult literacy educator. Ever since the 1970s, I have been involved in teaching, writing and researching with others in a kind of challenge to the fixed "great divide" view of literacy: the "either–or" view that says either you can read and write or you can't; either a society is civilised or it is illiterate (as discussed in the work of Brian Street, see Bibliography). One day, when I was researching for a book taking another slant on this topic – to explore how the old practice of scribing still features, almost unnoticed, in so many social relationships today – I was talking with my friend Caroline Nursey. She asked me if I had heard of the Quaker way of clerking business meetings. No, I said. A few weeks later, at her invitation, I sat in a meeting house participating in a Quaker meeting for worship for business, and there, as she had told me I would, I witnessed a scribe at work: a Quaker clerk.

It was the first time I had seen anything like it. As in countless other meetings I had been to over the years, there were copies of an agenda on every seat; but there the resemblance ended. The meeting began in silence. The clerk introduced each item. There were questions and comments. Then, at a certain moment, with all others present waiting in silence, the clerk and her assistant began writing. After a few moments she looked up and, from the file she held open in front of her, read out what she had written so far, looked up, asked "Is that acceptable?" and sat down. Individuals in the group, one, then another, offered a couple of small amendments. The clerk then conferred with her assistant again and wrote a little more. Once again she looked up and read aloud – this time a slightly revised version of the same text. Once again she asked if it was acceptable. This time the group murmured assent. For each subsequent item on the agenda they repeated the same pattern: introduction, discussion, pause, waiting as the clerk wrote, listening to the draft, and ensuring it was acceptable.

That visit told me how it was possible for someone to be supported as the writer of minutes in a business meeting. I wondered what this would look like to those I had taught in adult literacy classrooms during the 1970s and 80s. I remembered Mel, who had said: "I won't be going to that meeting, no. They might ask me to do the minutes."

I thought of Frank, who said: "You won't catch me in there. I'm not going to be made to look a fool." Mel and Frank: mature, skilful adults, for whom meetings meant keeping quiet in case someone "found them out", and for whom both writing and reading meant struggling on their own, feeling slow when others were fast. In this meeting they would have seen collaboration, time and company. Instead of the individual who had got "landed" with the job of minutes secretary for the local tenants' association, parents' meeting or church organisation, having to struggle with the spelling and word-choice there or later at home, the clerk had an assistant; and the meeting was there to wait, to look after them and to agree then and there the wording they came up with.

Over the next few years, I began attending Quaker meetings for worship, entered into membership, experienced the role of clerk at first hand, and wanted to know more.

The research proposal I set out in 2010 (for which Woodbrooke Quaker Study Centre in Birmingham granted me an Eva Koch award) had the focus of clerking and minute-writing. I asked: "How does it work? How does it vary?" What the one-year period of study I was given enabled me to do was move out to deeper waters – to the religious aspirations for making decisions, and the process by which Quakers seek to achieve them. The aim of this book is to share something of the rich array of experience I have been able to gather as a result.

This book

As I have said, many voices and experiences contributed to this book, and to all of them I feel grateful. You will find the resulting material organised in six interconnected areas: worship and time; discipline and upholding; unity and discernment; clerks and clerking; reading and writing; learning and communicating.

Although I have tried to write so that there is development through the book, you may prefer to see the six sections as six essays, more or less standing on their own. You are, of course, free to choose your own way in and out of the whole.

Introduction

1. Worship, God and time

Liberal Quakers have quite a range of ideas about what the word "God" means, and yet at the same time, while Quakers are making decisions the claim is that this is done through the search for God's will. Through vignettes of meetings for worship for business, I explore insights around this idea and some of the tensions it can raise in terms of timing.

2. Discipline and upholding

Upholding the clerk is something every meeting is asked to do. At the same time, Quakers ask themselves to apply a corporate discipline of waiting and listening. How do these activities become real in large gatherings and in small? To explore this, the chapter contains a close look at a session of Yearly Meeting and a business meeting in a small local meeting.

3. Unity and discernment

At the heart of the Quaker approach to decision-making is a commitment to find a unity that surpasses either consensus or vote. This is a unity grounded in divine guidance. Sometimes the sense of unity may be arrived at in a short space of time; at other times it may take a series of processes. For discernment to be achieved, examples of threshing meetings suggest these as a useful tool.

4. Clerks and clerking

This chapter sets out some of the thinking and experience of current clerks in meetings large and small in regard to spiritual preparation, drafting minutes and sharing the work. There are examples of the process of speech, writing and silence that clerks are asked to facilitate and "read", and clerkly strategies to rein in spoken contributions to allow for stillness. From a survey of current practice, I look at the benefits of co-clerking as a pattern of work for both individuals and meetings.

5. Reading and writing

In this chapter, I look at how Quakers use reading and writing in decision-making through the lens of a "social practice" view of literacy. The Quaker style of writing in our minutes is apparently simple, using active, personal and present-tense forms. The "literacy practices" of business meetings include an unusual commitment to reading aloud. This chapter explores what these practices might indicate in terms of values and meaning and considers the potential they hold for inclusivity.

6. Learning

How can a curious individual find out more? As a religious organisation committed to sustainability and a welcome to all, Quaker life offers various opportunities for informal learning and renewal. This last chapter offers examples of these. In a concluding note we are reminded of the limits of the written record, not least when God is in the process.

Quaker faith & practice

This is a key text that I will be referring to regularly throughout this book. The contents integrate sections on church organisation and the principles and practice of the faith with others on personal experiences of religious discoveries and spiritual journeys. It contains guidance and information about the structure of the organisation, the appointment of elders, arrangements for marriage, and so on. It is also an anthology of extracts from the work of Quaker writers over a period of more than three hundred and fifty years. A work about both Quaker theology and liturgy, it is the most recent form of the "book of discipline", containing the authority of the Society as a community. The last full revision was accepted by Yearly Meeting in 1994, after an appointed group of Friends were given the task of discerning what should go in it, and in what order. Sections dealing with the organisation are amended from time to time: the fourth edition of *Quaker faith & practice* (2009) includes revisions up to 2008.

Introduction

In terms of the literacy practice I discuss in Chapter 5, this is an unusual text for a religious organisation, combining as it does a mix of corporate and personal authorships (sections with no authors provide guidance to the organisation and the faith; sections with named authors offer personal witness to it) and being subject to regular revisions. Quakers draw on it both for personal sources of wisdom and encouragement and for guidance on procedure and discipline.

A note on terminology

Quakers use the word "meeting" to mean two things: an event and a community – and sometimes both at once. This book follows the style of Britain Yearly Meeting publications, using a capital M for Meeting only when it is a specifically named meeting.

Quaker structure

The Religious Society of Friends has a structure, within which the business goes on. The diagram on the next page shows the structure of Britain Yearly Meeting and where the local and area meetings fit within it.

Acknowledgements

My first thanks go to my own Quaker meeting in Gloucestershire and to the many Friends there who may not even know the various inspirations they give to me and no doubt many others. I owe thanks to Woodbrooke Quaker Study Centre, and especially to the Eva Koch award, which gave me the conditions and the permission to spend a year thinking about this most interesting area. Thanks also to the many Friends who allowed me to interview them, and in particular to Deborah Rowlands for being a thoroughly generous mentor, companion and reader along the research journey.

Thanks too to the hospitality of meetings visited: Central Edinburgh Local Meeting (LM), Bury St Edmunds LM, Milford Haven LM, Coventry LM, Kingston & Wandsworth AM, Gloucestershire AM;

GOD AND DECISION-MAKING

Young Friends General Meeting, Quakers Uniting in Publications, Yearly Meeting Gathering 2011 – and to the total of ninety-seven respondents to the three questionnaires undertaken around the experience of clerking and business meetings. Thanks also to Peter Daniels for his skill and care as copy editor, enabling this book to gain a good deal more flow than it had when it first reached him.

Finally I give thanks for the gradual revelation that this study enabled me to experience: namely, that the primary purpose of Quaker business meetings is not to make decisions or written records, but to seek (and sometimes find) a divine presence in the way these are made.

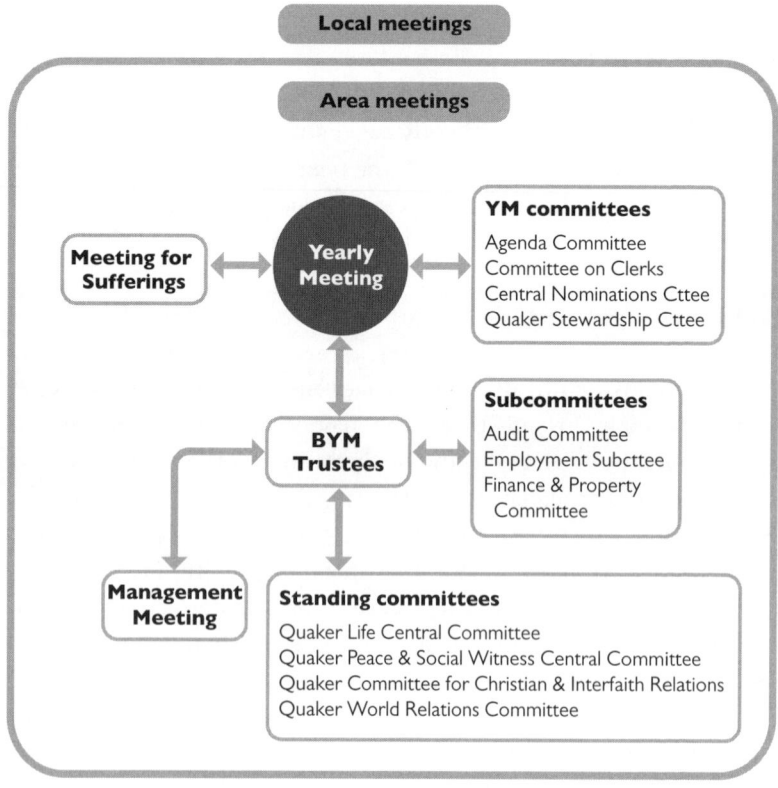

CHAPTER 1:

Worship, God and time

Worship, God and time

It seems clear that any attempt to understand the Quaker approach to making decisions needs to begin with a look at Quaker understandings of God. There is variety in Quaker usage of this word. As we shall see, when Quakers refer to "God", they do not always or automatically mean deity, let alone the divine as patriarch or saviour. As a Quaker myself, I find the wording "that of God" very helpful, offering a usage of the word "God" that suggests "essential goodness" as a meaning. (Frequently quoted today, the phrase originates in a message from George Fox to early Quakers, see *Qf&p* 19.32.) Giving recognition to that essential goodness, and the potential for it, is central to my effort to live the faith.

Meanwhile, as soon as we consider that the main forum for Quaker decision-making is a meeting for worship for business, we can imagine that there might be a possible contradiction to be faced. Business activity assumes values of efficiency and speed. Worship, on the other hand, does not. In this chapter, first through published Quaker writing and then through the experience of four meetings for worship for business, we explore two questions:

- what do Quakers mean by "seeking God's will" in their business meetings? and
- how do Quakers reconcile the demands of worship time and business time?

I will then consider these further through the experience of four meetings for worship for business.

God

At national level, when Britain Yearly Meeting is in session as the body with "ultimate authority for church affairs for Quakers in Britain" (*Qf&p* 6.12 and 8.01), its purpose is to "seek to hear the true word of God speaking through our frail humanity" (*Qf&p* 6.09). At local level, on a smaller scale, Quakers in meetings for worship for business – or for "church affairs" – do exactly the same. *Quaker faith & practice* sets out the idea like this:

> In our meetings for worship, we seek through the stillness to know God's will for ourselves and for the gathered group. Our meetings for church affairs, in which we conduct our business, are also meetings for worship based on silence, and they carry the same expectation that God's guidance can be discerned if we are truly listening together and to each other, and are not blinkered by preconceived opinions (*Qf&p* 3.02).

In short: for Quakers, making decisions involves an active search for divine leading.

But there is another word problem here. My earlier example of "essential goodness" as a Quaker usage of the word "God" does not altogether fit. How do we reconcile "God's will" and "divine guidance" with an abstract idea like that of "goodness"? (How can "goodness" have a will or give guidance?) As a glimpse of current Quaker thinking about this, the following extracts offer explorations of this question from three recent Swarthmore lectures, organised by Woodbrooke Quaker Study Centre and given during Yearly Meeting.

First, from a lifetime experience of both Quaker and Anglican religions, Beth Allen suggests the possibilities of reconciling a personal with an abstract idea of the divine. She notes the difficulty felt by many Quakers about God language, and links it to "our passionate search for truthfulness and integrity in our thought and speech". As she sees it, Quakers who are non-theists, trying out new ways to express inner experience, are part of the traditional Quaker commitment to truth. Her own usage of the word "God", she says, is

> as a shorthand for all the poetic, philosophical and imaginative things that have been said and written about a divinity at once elusive but knowable, with us and beyond us, communicable but also beyond words (Allen 2007, p. 15).

To a Quaker who does not find the personal God meaningful, this usage has appeal. It celebrates a divine mystery. Later in the same lecture, illustrating her view that the personal and the abstract can be merged, Beth Allen refers to God as "respecting the processes of our life", suggesting the divine as a person, or mind. At the same time, she evidently felt amused by a comment given to her by another Friend, that the phrase "God's will" seemed to imply "this awkward character, God, who knows the answer, but for some reason won't tell us what it is". More useful, she suggests, is to understand the idea of "God's will" as referring to the *process* of searching, not the answers sought (p. 41).

At Yearly Meeting a year later, lecturing on the subject of stewardship, Christine Davis explored the combined issues of how Quakers inherit and learn from their past and how they use words to communicate and express our deeper selves. Quakers, she says, are very concerned to describe what they *do*, but are less eager to explain *why they do it* – to describe their relationship with the divine (Davis 2008, p. 41). For her, the fact that Quakers have no common definition of "God" is a strength, "for words can never be adequate". However, she argues, if Quakers are to talk about the ground of their faith, they must be willing to share their various understandings. In her case, she tells us, when she uses the word "God", she finds there to be a strong sense of "the divine and the numinous", and of there being "a longer time frame than I can imagine". At the same time, she cannot herself imagine God in human terms. Rather, she pictures a brilliantly-faceted diamond, shimmering with light,

> the light is of love, a power which warms us as we share it, but is cold when solely self-centred (Davis 2008, pp. 24–25).

The following year, Peter Eccles (like Christine Davis, a former Yearly Meeting clerk) gave his lecture on the subject of discernment: how Quakers understand and use their decision-making process in a way that recognises "the presence in the midst". The guidance for business meetings, he points out, contains repeated references to "God". So, if Quakers want to think about their decision-making processes, they cannot avoid giving some thought to what this word means.

It is understandable, says Peter Eccles, that when humans wanted to imagine a deity behind the history of the universe, they felt the need to represent it in the most complex organism they could think of at the time: the human mind. However, while this idea seems to offer a profound comment on the universe, he could not himself accept the idea of God "the designer". Rather, as he puts it:

> God is a Spirit, not a Mind, an all-pervasive creative force at work in the universe ... [and] our spiritual awareness means that God, this creative force, "the ground of our being", acts through us and indeed anything of value that we do is a reflection of this creative force (Eccles 2009, pp. 52–53).

Living in God's presence, he goes on, means coming to meeting for worship and maintaining an awareness of the Spirit within us – the Reality.

This re-visioning of the idea of God, not as a planning mind but rather an energising spirit, seems to me to add a helpful female aspect to the idea. As I grew up in an Anglican tradition before women priests, God had always been shown to me as an external male, if not patriarchal, figure, leaving out of possibility anything I could contribute. The language of the liturgy had seemed to insist on a Lord and Father who knew my heart and mind better than I could. With the alternative voices of 1970s feminism, women of my generation began to see and hear female authority – and even divinity – reclaiming its place, and to find our own place within it. Peter Eccles' note on this offers a connection with that, I think, as does the general Quaker view of equality around ministry, which offers a liberation to all – and women especially, I suspect – who first experience it. Not, it should be noted, that Quakers have always and consistently felt an equal balance between women and men in their practice. As Ursula O'Shea points out, after the early promise of equality among 17th-century Quakers, things became more restricted over time, and it was not until 1918 that a woman first served as clerk of London Yearly Meeting (O'Shea 2003, p. 57).

Like Christine Davis, I do not find the phrase "seeking the will of God" useful, and perhaps this is because of a lingering association of "will" with masculine mastery. For her (holding on to her image of a scintillating diamond), rather we are "seeking to fulfil the loving purposes of God". "Both, of course, contain that difficult word 'God'", she says:

but for me, the important shift is between "the will" which implies finality and "loving purposes" which gives room for continuing exploration and development. It also allows the method of exploration to become part of the loving purposes themselves (Davis 2008, p. 54).

For those with a literal turn of mind, this might feel like an irritating rather than helpful construction; for how can a diamond have a purpose? With a more poetic approach, however, we could accept that this is metaphor at work – and as such allow it to take us to a deeper layer of understanding and acceptance.

With that in mind, let us now turn to the reality of trying to conduct an "efficient" business meeting in a worshipful manner – and to the tricky issue of time.

Worship

In meetings for worship, Quakers worship as equals, in stillness and in trust. As with the word "God", this seems to add a different meaning to another word in common use. "Worship" is often taken to imply a subject being venerated or prayed to. In a Quaker context, however, it seems to be most often used to mean an exercise of the spirit, with no evident object in mind. During the meeting, participants may be led to stand and "minister", but for a good part of the time no-one utters a word: the primary aim being for those present to find a "gathered stillness".

This is how meetings for worship are explained to visitors on the website of Quakers in Britain:

> A Quaker meeting creates a space of gathered stillness. We come together where we can listen to the promptings of truth and love in our hearts, which we understand as rising from God. Our meetings are based on silence: a silence of waiting and listening. Most meetings last for about an hour.
>
> The silence is different from the silence of solitary meditation, as the listening and waiting in a Quaker meeting is a

shared experience in which worshippers seek to experience God for themselves. The seating is usually arranged in a circle or a square to help people be aware of one another and conscious of the fact that they are worshipping together as equals. There are no priests or ministers.

The silence may be broken if someone present feels called to say something which will deepen and enrich the worship. Anyone is free to speak, pray or read aloud if they feel strongly led to do so. This breaks the silence for the moment but does not interrupt it.

In the quietness of the meeting, we can become aware of a deep and powerful spirit of love and truth, transcending our ordinary, day-to-day experiences. This sense of direct contact with the divine is at the heart of the Quaker way of worship and nourishes Quakers in the rest of their daily lives. (www.quaker.org.uk/what-happens-meeting-worship)

The stress on the difference between solitary and communal worship is a frequent theme in Quaker guidance. In the *Quaker faith & practice* section on "experience and nature of worship", for example:

True worship may be experienced at any time; in any place – alone on the hills or in the busy daily life – we may find God, in whom we live and move and have our being. But this individual experience is not sufficient, and in a meeting held in the Spirit there is a giving and receiving between its members, one helping another with or without words. So there may come a wider vision and a deeper experience (*Qf&p* 2.11).

Pierre Lacout's booklet *God is silence*, first published in French in 1969 and later translated and widely circulated in English, offers a helpful understanding of this form of religious practice. As he puts it, silence "is a way of seeing which needs no object". The group seated with heads bowed in a meeting for worship do not need an object for that worship. The silence they are creating "can only be defined as direction. It is a looking towards, not a looking at". "Ideas about God", he goes on,

> are good only if I move quickly on from them. The sweet savours coming from God are good only if we leap forward from them. We must always go beyond (Lacout 1969/2003, p. 13).

There is a series of stages that may occur in the journey through such silence, each one corresponding, says Lacout, to "a progress in love". First comes the start of the search, "active silence". Then follow the stages that are the gifts, he says, of God's grace: the grace of "inward retirement"; of "inward quiet"; of "union"; and finally, deepest of all, of "fusion" (p. 22). It seems likely that if this is the kind of worshipping that is desired, it needs work: for it to grow, it must be practised.

In a world in which efficiency is a first tenet of good business, Quakers aspire to *do* their business in a worshipful way. In arriving at a decision, the priority is to achieve a sense of rightness, of "divine guidance". The aim is to ground the process of decision-making in loving faith and practice. Meetings for worship for business (often known as "meetings for church affairs") are expected to be more than mere committees added on to the real work: they are required to be godly times.

For many years before coming to Quakers, a good part of my working life not only entailed attending meetings, but also supporting and teaching others to do so. In the world of adult literacy and community education during the 1970s and 80s, there was a great deal of effort put into ways and means of making learning participatory, and into linking learning with community life of one sort or another. The work of trade union educators had a big part to play. Inspired by the many determined people we met with, some of us published books and guidance about these things.

Anyone involved in the voluntary sector or in local organisations is all too likely to get mixed up in the work of constitutions, agendas and committees, quite apart from routine meetings that may come up in a working day. During the course of writing this book, I have had various conversations with Quaker and other friends about meetings of all sorts, at work or in community life. Everyone I spoke to commented on the differences they found between these and the business meetings that Quakers hold. Quakers talk of "considering" a topic. Elsewhere, people talk about "discussing" one. While Quakers expect to hear or to voice opinions, they attempt, at the same time, to ensure that there is a pause between these, even some time of silence. In other meetings, there will sometimes be quickfire interchange, two or three people speaking at once; if well chaired, there will be some reasoned argument and a vote, or an agreement of some sort, with the written minutes brought to the next meeting. In Quaker meetings, there is an idea of arriving at "unity" – rather than a majority, let alone unanimous decision – for which the group as a whole is expected to give acceptance by hearing read out a written record of the decision – before going on to the next topic on the agenda.

The following table seems to offer a useful summary of these differences, with Quaker-organised events aspiring, at least, to follow the pattern sketched down the left-hand column, and those that take place in other communities and organisations expected to follow the pattern sketched in the right-hand one.

	In Quaker meetings	In other meetings
Those present are seeking	God's will, unity	unanimous/majority decision or consensus
by means of	consideration and discernment	debate, discussion
guided by	the "presence in the midst", the Spirit, moments of attentive silence	opinion, evidence, rational argument

In the pattern sought by Quakers, in the context of busy lives, this suggests a problem: how to undertake this careful, considered discernment and get home in time for other commitments?

Time

Writing thirty years ago, Cecil Sharman's comments on this issue still ring true today:

> All Quaker meetings are subject to a contradiction. Their foundation is in the Spirit, in the waiting, and the unhurried seeking for the true way. But we exist in the material world. The life in the Spirit has to be reconciled with the weariness of the body, with meals, with buses, trains, closing car-parks, and crowded or foggy roads (Sharman 1983, p. 33).

To many people, both Quakers and others, the idea of a business meeting as a time for worship seems doomed to make the event very slow and long. Yet, as Christine Davis puts it, the Quaker concern lies elsewhere:

> When we are transacting business under religious concern – God's business, rather than the world's – we are not required to move at the pace which the world demands. Following the integrity of our religious leadings is our prime responsibility (Davis 2008, p. 62).

In meetings for worship for business, the idea is that those present wait to be called to speak by the clerk, ensure that there is a pause between each contribution and avoid any individual repeating contributions on the same subject. Most of all, there is an idea that time will be allowed for the Spirit to flow. We could call this an idea about "divine time" and it is one that requires a certain self-restraint.

In her study of how present-day Quakers make choices about time, Judy Frith reminds us that Quakers today live most of their lives in the secular world, with the usual clock time of diaries, deadlines, priorities dominating their days and weeks (Frith 2010). As an organisation, the structure and life of the Religious Society of Friends depends on a lot of time being "donated" by its adherents. Making connections between this "holy" or "Quaker" time and the clock variety presents pressures and a sense of "busyness" that may be at odds with a Quaker commitment to "wait on God". This all makes for a complex context, says Judy Frith, from which Quakers make choices about giving time to their worship community.

Attending a business meeting means "giving time", and meetings of any kind are notorious for going on too long. While Quaker business meetings are also meant to be occasions for worship, with a loving approach to decision-making, every Quaker will have a story of one where things did not go well, let alone "worshipfully". As *Quaker faith & practice* puts it, however, these events offer a chance to exercise the capacity for personal discipline: for these meetings are

> not merely occasions for transacting with proper efficiency the affairs of the church but also opportunities when we can learn to bear and forbear, to practise to one another that love which "suffereth long and is kind" (*Qf&p* 3.03).

The reminder of this loving purpose is made more than once in published guidance, together with a recognition of the "frailty" of human beings. Experience suggests that Quaker business meetings can often include times when participants feel impatient, bored or frustrated at how things are going. In the words of another Quaker writer, Nancy Krieger, it would be easy for a meeting to succeed if all present are feeling happy, intelligent and active, but no-one feels these things on a permanent basis:

> Unfortunately, most of us are, sometimes, immature, stumbling, grumbling, lazy, ordinary human beings. And with Quakers, each one has their own very special idea of just what should be done (Krieger 2009, p. 31).

The issue of time comes up in several ways. There is a felt need to balance a proper concern for religious faith and practice with a respect for other timetables. Local meetings advertise their weekly meetings for worship on noticeboards, with the times they start and finish. When it comes to business meetings, however, there are mixed feelings about whether to publish a time that a business meeting will finish. On the one hand, there is a view that "God will not be hurried", as Alan Russell wrote in a letter to *The Friend* (8 October 2010, p. 8). On the other, experience suggests that the small numbers at some business meetings may have something to do with an uncertainty as to how long the meeting will take.

One Sunday in October 2011, just before the start of the monthly business meeting of Kingston & Wandsworth Area Meeting, I overheard an example of this position. Meeting for worship was just over, with the business meeting due to start in half an hour. Friends were settling down to their sandwiches. Others were beginning to arrive and one was about to leave, saying he would not be joining us. "If I had known what time it was going to end, I would have come", he said. He went on to explain that he is the only Quaker in his household and the father of teenage children.

I would not risk generalising from the visits and interviews I have undertaken, but there does at least seem to be a school of thought among Quakers that knowing the end time of a meeting would encourage quite a few other Quakers to start attending. Yearly Meeting sessions are timetabled within a whole programme to show what time they finish as well as when they begin, but not usually local and area meetings for worship for business. Those present may be used to other committees in other contexts where they would grumble at one that went on "over time". Quaker meetings for worship for business, by contrast, seem generally expected to "take as long as they take". So it seems that a tension persists between what could be called the "divine timescale" and the human one. "Our local business meetings used to go on for hours", one Friend writes,

> so the clerk has worked hard to make sure business does not overrun – but this can sometimes feel against the Quaker way of worship.

Vignettes

Why do Quaker business meetings vary in quality? And what can be done about it when their quality is poor? These are the questions Robert Halliday set himself to explore for a George Gorman lecture at the 1989 Yearly Meeting in Aberdeen, published as *Mind the oneness*. From observation, reading and experience, his answer to the first question is discipline: not, he says, discipline as in deprivation ("cold showers, hard work and the bare minimum of spontaneous pleasure"); rather, discipline as in the commitment to learn, as a disciple learns, the discipline that early Quakers developed and required to ensure the gathered meeting be recognised as the source of authority, rather than the inspired individual.

The quality of a business meeting, he concludes, varies according to the quality of two main kinds of discipline being used by those taking part: their *personal* discipline and the *corporate* discipline of the assembled meeting. If the personal and corporate disciplines are observed, and the clerks manage the tasks of reading the sense of the meeting and capturing the essence of discernment in writing, then, says Halliday, the meeting is experienced as gathered.

"Discipline" in a Quaker business meeting is at one level a matter of behaviour. Quakers are known for being a "non-credal faith": that is, a faith that does not express itself through a creed, a written set of beliefs. But as Ben Pink Dandelion suggests, woven into the disciplines is an idea of what is acceptable that (while not being a list of rules) adds up to a kind of creed for how to behave. The example he gives is of the preferred style, timing and length of spoken ministry, written into *Quaker faith & practice*. This advisory stance on discipline he calls a "behavioural creed" (Dandelion 2005, p. 101). Before exploring this further, it seems timely to glimpse some Quaker business meetings in action.

Every month of every year, some five hundred local meetings across England, Wales and Scotland sit down and attempt to make decisions in a spirit of worship. They do this for anything between half an hour and three hours at a time. The seventy-odd area meetings, formerly called "monthly meetings", do the same thing, but today typically rather less than once a month, and for rather more than three hours.

There to seek not unanimity nor majority votes but "unity", participants in these meetings are asked to exercise a discipline that is more than simply behavioural: it is the capacity to accept a decision that they may have neither expected nor wanted, but trust to be the best one for the meeting at the time.

The meetings noted below as vignettes, or miniature samples of practice, took place on two consecutive weekends in March 2011. The vignettes are based on questionnaire responses I received after a letter of mine was published in the 25 February 2011 issue of *The Friend*. It was an invitation to readers to send in a "snapshot" of a recent meeting for worship for business they had attended.

I had grouped the questions in three sections:

- **Before the meeting:** details of the where, when, what and who of the meeting, together with a note on the respondent's experience of it;
- **During the meeting:** physical arrangements of the room, persons supporting the clerk, *the worship and discipline aspect of the meeting*, and the kinds of reading and writing that went on during it; and
- **After the meeting:** the respondent's observations of the spoken ministry, of the nature of the reading expected or read out and of the clerk's writing, and any general reflections on either the meeting or on the exercise of doing this recording.

By way of response, 17 Friends completed a total of 22 questionnaires. Each of these responses gave what a camera may provide: a snapshot, a glimpse of one event in the life of a meeting, which has had other experiences before this and will have others to come. In each of the vignettes, I have used the term "reporter" to refer to the Friend whose questionnaire response helped me to compose it.

In bare facts and figures, each of the 22 responses conjured up the glimpse of a business meeting at work. In order to consider something of the reality these may have felt like, I offer here four vignettes based on this basic data. (For their consent in using these, I am grateful to reporters Julia Aspden, Barbara Cairns, Adrienne Jeorrett, Alan Rowland, Jane Taylor and Fiona Waddington.)

1. Local meetings

1.1 The first of these two meetings, taking place on the same Sunday, is relatively large and lasts for nearly three hours. Its reporter notes that she has attended business meeting when childcare allowed, perhaps six times in the last two or three years.

> In a meeting house, **18 Friends** gather in a semicircle of chairs. Clerk and assistant sit at the table in front of them. At least one elder is present. The meeting starts with silence. Friends rise and wait for the clerk to invite them to speak with a nod or eye contact. There is a pause between contributions.
>
> On the whole the meeting is attentive; however, at one point the clerk "admonishes" some who are whispering and laughing, and at another a member of the meeting quietly tells a newish Friend to wait for the clerk to finish writing before making her point. For several items, the person presenting stands at the front and reads out a report.
>
> For the reporter, this feels about average, and she feels the meeting has been working with the clerk while they have drafted the minute.
>
> On reflection, she adds,
>
>> It felt a good meeting, because we managed to work through some difficult issues without too much tension... but also uncomfortable, because it was quite long and we forgot to have a shuffle break, which we try to have if it goes on a while.
>
> The whole meeting lasted **two hours and forty minutes**.

1.2 The second meeting is smaller and shorter. The reporter has been attending its sessions "for years". It is part of the habit of a lifetime; a routine among friends familiar to each other.

> In the town "activity centre", a small group (**six Friends**) meet for Quaker business straight after their weekly meeting for worship.

They sit in a horseshoe, with a gap in the centre. No-one present is designated as an elder; all but one are members of the meeting's "spiritual and pastoral care group". The meeting starts with a few moments of silence. One member acts as clerk. Anyone who has something to say does so from their seat.

The clerk writes notes as the discussion proceeds, reads out the first draft of a minute, to which one or two present offer minor amendments, and then reads out the second draft. Friends do not wait to be asked to speak, but respond to each other. One speaks several times.

The meeting seems to have satisfied the reporter; he comments:

We made the necessary decisions. Because we all know each other very well over many years, we perhaps rather disregard procedures necessary in a larger meeting.

The whole meeting lasted **half an hour**.

In the first meeting, the comment is mixed: it was good because they got through some difficult matters; it was not good because it was quite long without a break. It felt as if most present were attentive. There was a "pause between contributions". The whole meeting lasted nearly three hours, and in that kind of time energy may flag. As in any meeting, we can imagine there may be a regular core who come to every meeting; two or three who, like the reporter, come when they can; and perhaps one attending for the first time. Each will bring different levels of knowledge about the topics. To some, the meeting may have felt very long; to others, amazingly short.

The second meeting "made the necessary decisions" and disposed of its business in half an hour, and "perhaps disregarded" the usual disciplines – participants not leaving pauses between contributions, and one speaking "several times". For the reporter, the meeting felt satisfactory. Participants, as he put it, put to one side the "procedures" needed in a larger meeting. As Michael Booth comments, in his preface to the 2010 edition of Halliday's book:

> In my experience, smaller groups often find the Quaker business method harder to follow than larger ones (Halliday 2010, p. iv).

Two questions occur to me. Was it just because this second meeting had a fraction of the number present compared to the first one that it lasted so much less time – or were there other reasons? And what are the procedures necessary in a small meeting? If it is not "necessary" to stand up to speak, or wait for the clerk to give you the nod to speak, are there any reasons other than practical ones that make these practices useful for maintaining worship?

2. Area meetings

The following Saturday, two area meetings met.

2.1 In a meeting house, **34 people** attend this afternoon meeting. The room is so full that some Friends have to sit behind the clerk and assistant clerk, who face a three-sided square. The meeting begins with a longish silence. The reporter does not feel distracted by the clerk using a laptop to draft notes.

> The assistant clerk reads an extract from *Quaker faith & practice*, and stands up to do so. Almost without exception, anyone wanting to speak stands and waits to be called by the clerk. A pause follows almost all contributions. There is a lot to be read, but it all seems necessary. On two occasions there seems to be a need to remind Friends of how to behave. While the clerks are drafting a minute, the reporter herself feels this need: "Towards the end I did frown at the whispering behind me".
>
> And when one speaker seems to be going on too long, the clerk gives him an oblique reminder of right ordering. The

speaker is giving some kind of presentation to one agenda item and seems to come to a pause, though not the final end. At this point the clerk thanks him warmly and moves on to the next item of business.

For the reporter, this felt like a good meeting, because

> although it was a very long meeting it felt that it needed to be. Complex and delicate matters needed sensitive discernment. I felt that it was right that we weren't hurried. Under the circumstances I thought that Friends kept the discipline well. One might say that it became a little ragged at times towards the end, but actually that wouldn't be quite fair.

The meeting started at two o'clock. It closed at five past six.

2.2 In a rented conference room, **26 Friends** gather for a **day meeting**, timetabled to allow an hour for lunch in the middle. The body of the meeting is arranged in rows facing the clerk's table where the clerk, assistant clerk and two appointed elders sit. The meeting begins with half an hour of silence, with a reading from *Advices & queries* in the middle.

> Several agenda items have letters or reports to be read out loud and readers come to the front of the meeting to do this. Before speaking, Friends stand and wait for the clerk to call them. There are no interruptions. The meeting is quiet while the clerks draft the minute.

For the reporter

> It felt like a good meeting because there were several attenders present and one of them came into membership. The meeting was well planned and well spaced out. We had a shuffle break when necessary. There seemed to be no unnecessary business and what there was, was interesting.

In response to one question, "does anyone (if so, who?) remind the meeting in general of an aspect of right ordering?", the reporter responded:

> It was the clerk who did the reminding. A Friend was waffling rather, and the clerk interrupted and suggested that this was something that could be discussed over lunch, but did not in fact have to be considered at this point in the agenda.

Both of these meetings began in silence. In the first, the reporter judged that one speaker went on "too long", and appreciated the strategy used by the clerk to interrupt and end their contribution. The meeting as a whole lasted just over four hours, but on this the reporter made no complaints, judging that the matters needed the time and Friends appreciated not being hurried.

The mention of the "appointed elders" in the second account prompted me also to ask the reporter about their role in "reminding", since almost no other respondents had mentioned elders taking a role in the meeting. This was her reply:

> The two appointed elders for the meeting sit at the table for the initial period of silence, but then take places in the main body of Friends. We are trying to ensure that the appointed elders know that they have responsibility for the right ordering of the meeting, but I'm afraid very often they don't remember this.

These vignettes of larger (area) meetings raise two more questions. With whom lies the care of the discipline – with clerks or with elders? As other respondents noted, the "reminding" of respectful behaviour can as well come from an experienced participant in the meeting as from either elder or clerk, and the spiritual care of the meeting is indeed the responsibility of elders. Several other reporters also noted, however, that elders themselves may sometimes forget the corporate discipline.

Secondly: while the clerk's planning of the meeting's business can anticipate the need for breaks, how can they also plan for silence? Even with the best-planned agendas, Friends forget the discipline.

Worship, God and time

What many respondents noted is that the holding of this discipline needs to be the responsibility of others as well as the clerk, not least the elders.

There is, of course, something more than the clock time of a meeting that can make it feel long. A two-hour meeting in one place can fly by; another meeting of the same length can feel like an eternity. Timing, in the end, is a matter of respect and discipline in its fullest sense. If a meeting goes on so long that energies have gone, there is no longer much hope of feeling "gathered". Meetings seem too often to be extended when a discussion goes off at a tangent, cutting the time left to fully explore another agenda item. Reporting on a meeting that she felt had been too long (two and three-quarter hours instead of the usual two hours), one reporter complained:

> A long discussion about ways of giving (through collections, individually or by local meeting) should have been curtailed, as there were two major items on the agenda and not time to deal with them adequately. The long discussion degenerated into conversations with the treasurer rather than addressing the meeting.

Clerk training teaches that matters that are likely to attract a lot of discussion may best be deferred until after the meeting, or to the work of another group. What comes with practice is the confidence to draw on the authority that the meeting gives the clerk to take the lead in the meeting itself and to tell Friends that this matter "needs more work than we have allowed for it here". As you would expect, *Quaker faith & practice* offers measured advice on this (see 3.06 on unity and 13.05 on discernment in concern).

Afterword

To resolve the tensions between worship and business, Cecil Sharman takes a firm approach:

> If the Life is not to be stifled, time must not be wasted.

In every moment of the session self-discipline is needed (Sharman 1983, p. 33).

For the clerk, he says, there is a calculation that can be made. If there are two hours available for the meeting, six major matters on the agenda, and twenty small housekeeping jobs to be covered, just add three minutes to each of the six items and one minute to each of the twenty, and you will have added the "serious overrun" of forty minutes to your intended two-hour session.

His list of suggestions for saving "the little moments that so swiftly add up" includes, first, these – for all participants in the meeting:

- each statement: make once and once only
- everybody speak "briskly", not with "apologetic slowness and needless qualifications"
- "shun narrative and circumstantial detail" – i.e. cut waffle

He advises clerks to keep pauses short, both between speakers and after reading out a draft minute; to draw attention to progress throughout the agenda ("chide, congratulate, or commiserate as required") and to "urge Friends through the formalities with the carrot that they will then have leisure to expand over some interesting speculative topic".

While the picture he draws may be a little old-fashioned (who "chides" today?), Cecil Sharman's wisdom endures, not least the advice to the clerk to tell the meeting at the start what time it will end, and – "unless there is some overwhelming and unforeseeable difficulty" – to keep "strictly to this indicated timing", remembering "those who have children waiting for them, appointments or shift-times to keep, invalids to assist, babysitters to release". At the same time, "if the Life is not to be stifled" and the Spirit given space, the clerk and the meeting together also need somehow to allow time for stillness, for words to sink in. In the biblical phrase familiar to some from a hymn (by the 19th-century Quaker poet John Greenleaf Whittier), there needs to be enough quiet to hear the "still, small voice of calm" (*Qf&p* 20.03).

For Quaker meetings to arrive at unity, those present have to feel a confidence in having been heard. This, in turn, takes a commitment to a mutual discipline. Because of familiarity and a greater sense of intimacy than is possible with more people present, small meetings may risk falling short on the corporate discipline necessary to achieve a full sense of being "gathered". In the next chapter, I will consider how – despite great differences between the small and the very large meeting – the importance of upholding corporate discipline and a worshipful approach remains the same in meetings of any size.

CHAPTER 2:

Discipline and upholding

Discipline and upholding

Between the early 1980s and mid-1990s, several guides and papers were published on Quaker decision-making (more often referred to as "the business method"), bringing together a combination of history and advice. This chapter looks at how some British and American Quaker sources consider the relationship between discipline and the search for unity, and at how the concept of "upholding" helps an understanding of the worshipping work of participants in business meetings. Then I explore disciplined worship in two kinds of meeting, very large and very small, and the creative paradox – formal and informal, public and private – that occurs in different-sized meetings.

Discipline

First published in 1983, Michael Sheeran's book about Quaker ways of using "communal discernment" draws on his research with Philadelphia Yearly Meeting. A Jesuit priest, he combines history and sociology in his approach to the subject. In Part 1, he tells the story of Quaker history from mid-17th to early 20th centuries; in Part 2, he sets out the "contemporary" situation. He shows how the concept of "discipline" is a constant for three hundred years: from the introduction to the *Advices* issued by the elders of Balby in 1656 to the 1960 London Yearly Meeting version of what has been generically called the "Book of discipline" (at that time two volumes, *Christian faith and practice* and *Church government*). Michael Sheeran also offers interesting comments on the leadership role of the clerk, noting a potential for clerks to abuse that power – through manipulating the minute or "reading the meeting" in a way that favours their own view. He explains the difference between the search for unity in Quaker meetings and the mistake of expecting these to follow a democratic way of making decisions. To avoid this mistake, he says, there is a need to enter into the Quaker "thought-world" (Sheeran 2nd ed 1996, p. 101).

A few years later, an American Quaker pamphlet on the principle of "gospel order" was published. Early Quakers used this term to refer to the acceptable practices of worship, decision-making and daily living in Quaker meetings. In her discussion of this, Sandra Cronk says that it was (and still is) the dynamic of "mutual accountability" (sometimes called "church discipline") that kept gospel order strong; providing a means to reconcile inward life and social concern (Cronk 1991, pp. 16–21).

Robert Halliday's findings, introduced in the last chapter, were published in the same year as Sandra Cronk's pamphlet. For meetings for worship for business to go well, he reports, discipline needs to be in active use – both personal and corporate. Quakers express this discipline through certain ways of behaving:

> sitting in a circle or square, not speaking unless called by the clerk, rising to speak, drafting and approving the minute during the meeting, maintaining a worshipful silence while the clerk prepares the minute, speaking briefly unless the subject really demands it, not repeating what has been said before and addressing the meeting as a whole rather than one particular Friend (Halliday 1991, p. 49).

For such discipline to be valued and sustained, he suggests three elements that help: that those present should, first, know the Spirit; second, know each other; and third, know the methods. Handing on the traditions in a loving way, creating opportunities to get together as a community, worshipping together – these activities can support the meeting to recognise and put corporate discipline to best use.

In the work of two other writers from the same period, Barry Morley and Patricia Loring, I found interesting insights on what participants in the meeting for worship for business could be doing – apart from modifying behaviour in outward, disciplined ways. Both write about how the disciplined search for unity should be a matter not merely of the clerk's skills and gifts, but of what I see as the whole meeting's *spiritual effort*. Between them, they offer two tools to help build a sense of a collective at work. The first is the idea of taking a *long focus*; the second is that of not just one or two people doing the work of clerks, but of *everyone clerking*.

A long focus

"Corporate decisions" in Quaker life have nothing to do with

Discipline and upholding

consensus, let alone democracy. In *Beyond consensus: salvaging sense of the meeting*, Barry Morley describes how this was the message he found himself having to repeat over and over again in his years of work as Quaker school teacher, camp director, and member of Baltimore Yearly Meeting in America. The Quaker commitment is not to a secular consensus but to the "sense of the meeting", an idea derived, he says, from the commitment of early Quakers to continuing revelation, as opposed to sudden and singular moments of discovery. "Through consensus we decide it; through sense of the meeting we turn it over, allowing it to be decided", he writes, quoting another Friend's comment: "Reaching consensus is a secular process … In sense of the meeting, God gets a voice" (Morley 1993, p. 5). In order for this alternative process to be achieved, the meeting needs to focus its attention beyond the immediate discussion *towards* this sense. And for that to happen, Morley suggests, three overlapping components are essential: release, a long focus, and transition to Light.

Release may first occur when the clerk or another participant presents an issue to the meeting. Friends who have strong feelings on the matter release their feelings or opinions on it – fear, opposition, irritation or excitement, for example. The stage, says Morley, is an important one, with "tender attentiveness" being the meeting's gift. However, for the meeting to remember the sense of the whole on the matter being considered, this attentiveness needs to be not only on the speaker's feelings but also on the object of the meeting.

Opinions and competing ideas, as he notes, have the effect of "shortening focal length" (p. 17); personal needs and grievances, likewise. So the focus then needs to move from a shortened focus on strong feelings to a longer one; having made time for a period of release, the meeting needs to pull back, as it were, to gain this broader perspective. If so led, someone will stand to speak in a way that helps this to happen. If they do not, a vigilant clerk may remind the meeting of the task and ask for a "refocus" on it.

In short, he suggests, what needs to happen is a move from release towards transition to Light, via a move from short to long focus:

From the Light we sense an influx of enveloping harmony.

> Peace tinged with triumph settles upon individuals and over the meeting. When we feel the Presence settle among us, and silence overtakes us, we have arrived where we want to be (p. 19).

It is through a process of allowing all these three stages to occur – release of first feelings and opinions, a long focus beyond these and a turning towards the Light – that a gathered group may find revealed a true "sense of the meeting".

Since I read and considered this portrayal of the collective work of the group, I have sometimes sat in meetings where a sequence like this does indeed seem to occur (an example of which we shall look at shortly). In the next chapter's discussion on discernment, we will consider a slightly different view of a discerning process – not from release to Light, but from rational discourse to divine guidance when the focus may be broad as well as long.

Everyone clerking

Discerning is difficult; it is not infallible; it is fragile; and it is not just the clerk's job to worry about it. This is the message Patricia Loring offers in the second volume of *Listening spirituality*, which is called *Corporate spiritual practice among Friends*. There often seems a danger in Quaker life, she suggests, that we expect those Friends appointed to serve as clerks to do all the work for the meeting, and like Barry Morley she offers a powerful alternative to the idea of a collective at work. In her book, she writes that while clerks may be the "designated discerners" of the meeting, they are not the only ones. Certainly, they may have been appointed for their gifts of discernment, she goes on, but "that does not mean that the rest of the meeting relinquishes the task of discernment" to them:

> Knowing the difficulty, fallibility and fragility of discernment, it is their task to support the clerk's discernment in whatever manner seems to be required in particular instances to the best of their capacities. *It's axiomatic that the clerk clerks best when everyone is clerking together* (Loring 1997, p. 91; my italics).

Discipline and upholding

This is the business meeting as a collective, at work on a shared task, in which the one who, for the time being, is acting as the conduit for discernment, as it were, does that best when the rest of the group "to the best of their capacities" support him or her in that role. They may not be drafting the minute; they may not be speaking; but as attentive listeners – attentive to the Spirit as well as the words – they are all clerks.

Like Robert Halliday, Patricia Loring sees the personal and corporate disciplines as interdependent. As she points out, we each bring our spiritual lives into the group meeting. The vignettes in the last chapter gave numbers, not names: but for each Friend present, there too is a spiritual life, to be listened to and to share. A central feature of corporate spirituality, says Loring, is the practice of corporate listening; listening, that is, for the Spirit among us, "to move past ... sweetness and light" (p. 8), as she puts it, into recognition of our human differences, struggles and pain – finding the discipline to be able to participate with people who irritate us, and in so doing make a possible contribution to our spiritual growth.

The most recent published discussion I have found on Quaker decision-making is in Derrick Whitehouse's workbook and workshop materials on "the relevance and implementation of Gospel Order", *Towards an inspired Quaker meeting*. In an interesting chapter on "Working on the meeting culture", the author offers what he calls his own version of "worship and process". Unlike other writers, he prefers the term "etiquette" to "discipline", saying that "worship, etiquette and process" are the three key elements that Quakers seek to hold together in their decision-making. For the worship and discernment to go well, he recommends that every individual is "aware of the stage that a particular issue is at in the process", adding:

> I believe that the most essential part of the procedure is to provide space in the conduct of the discernment ... for the sense of worship and the etiquette to be truly felt and meaningful (Whitehouse 2009, p. 66).

Because, as he puts it, "holding a stance of worship for some time can be emotionally taxing", he has a direct solution to the tension between worship time and clock time. "I am pursuing a personal campaign", he writes,

> for well constructed short agenda where the Quaker business method can flourish and be enjoyed (p. 68).

Upholding

In the *Quaker faith & practice* guidance on the relationship between the meeting and its clerks, there is certainly an emphasis on active participation. The relationship with the clerk (or clerks) is expressed as one of "upholding", which the meeting should do at two moments. The first is when clerks are trying to resolve conflict:

> We have a responsibility to uphold our clerks in prayer as they try to discern unity in sharply divided meetings (*Qf&p* 3.07).

The second is when a clerk is in the process of drafting a minute:

> If, when all that is necessary has been said, the clerk is not ready to submit a minute, uphold those at the table in prayerful silence (*Qf&p* 3.11).

What is upholding? How do Quakers offer it to each other, as well as to the clerk? If the meeting's intention is to seek unity, divine guidance, God's will, then should all be upholding something else – a sense of common purpose, perhaps? This kind of discipline is a commitment not only to listen attentively and, when appropriate, to voice concerns and difference, but also to accept and trust that between those present, the group can manage to get to a decision that is right for the collective. "Upholding the meeting" could be a way to express it.

The Yearly Meeting session described shortly in this chapter required, in my own case, an exercise of discipline from which I learned something of this "upholding" and in so doing discovered what unity might feel like. Looking back later, I saw the part that

Discipline and upholding

the clerk, Lis Burch, played in enabling that discovery. During the course of the seven Yearly Meeting sessions, we had seen and heard her at other times "call us to order". In the session you are about to find described, she both led the discipline and admonished the meeting for falling short of its demands. During this session, I found myself stirred by a sense of having something urgent to say, but was not given the chance to say it. In summary, this is what took place:

> The clerk had just read out to us the draft minute. She sat down, and one by one individuals in the gathering wishing to contribute to this stood up, waiting to be called to speak. During the total of thirty minutes that followed, I was one of the many others who stood and did not get the clerk's eye. In all, during that time, I think I stood up and sat down again perhaps seven times – my unspoken ministry thumping away in my chest, remaining essentially the same, but slightly changing as I listened to the other speakers. I was feeling increasingly agitated. The contributions did not seem to be addressing the question. One or two seemed to me to be assuming an "us-and-them" position about inequality, injustice, and action being taken about them. I wanted to speak out about Quakers as Friends in work, living unheard testimony that we ought to be listening out for. I felt full of words, but the meeting's disciplines held me quiet, and each time I sat down in slow motion and listened to someone else.
>
> And then a curious thing happened. Just before the last speaker was heard, I found the urgency at not being heard and the irritation at what others were saying had simply ebbed away. When the clerk finally stood up and read out a draft of the completed minute, I felt at peace.

Some days later, I made a list of the spiritual and mental exercises I had found myself going through in that half an hour, having to:

- keep my mind on the topic
- listen to other speakers

- appreciate the silence in the pauses
- question my own leadings, and
- accept not being heard.

For me, these active and conscious efforts of mind, heart and spirit seemed to be what "upholding" might mean. My reward, at the time, was the sense of unity that unfolded. I would like to consider now how some of this discipline and upholding seems to occur in large and small meetings. The first is the aforementioned session of the Religious Society of Friends in Britain's Yearly Meeting Gathering 2011 at Canterbury. The second is a meeting for worship for business at Milford Haven Quaker Meeting.

Large

The activity most participants undertake during a yearly meeting in session is to sit and say nothing. Outwardly, those present could appear to be rows and rows of passive onlookers, while the clerks work at the table on the platform and the invited few among the hundreds of seated Friends stand up in turn to say their piece.

A classic session opens with ten minutes of worship. The clerk then stands to introduce the session and reminds us of our task and (if necessary) of our discipline. They or another will then present the first matter. After they have sat down, those Friends who feel they have something to say will stand and wait to be called. After each contribution, the clerk may wait before calling on the next speaker, holding pauses of varying length. Eventually, after a certain number of speakers, the clerk may comment, offer a summary, ask for guidance, or simply call for quiet while they draft a minute. After a few moments, they will stand and offer this aloud to the meeting and then sit to see if there are any requests for any words or phrases to be added, left out, or changed. One or two Friends may in turn stand to make these suggestions. Again, the clerk may confer with the assistant or co-clerk to produce a redraft, then rise and read out an alternative version. If this is accepted, the meeting moves on to the next item.

All this sounds very much like one of the local or area meetings described earlier. However, because of the scale of the event and

Discipline and upholding

the number of participants, the disciplines of waiting and taking turns are that much more evident. What I have picked out from this example are two clerkly activities that also occur on a smaller scale: namely, capturing the minute and teaching the discipline.

On Tuesday 2 August 2011, Yearly Meeting's third session had one major item to consider: economic justice. By 9.30 that morning, when the clerks took their seats at the table, between eight and nine hundred of us were already seated in the huge blue circus tent in which all the sessions took place that week, and worship began. After fifteen minutes (during which there were four spoken ministries), the clerk rose to begin the business. After welcoming Friends, she asked the assistant clerk to read out, by way of opening ministry for the business, the epistle from Ramallah Friends Meeting (which we had already received on paper in our *Documents in advance*). He duly read out this text to the meeting. After a pause, the clerk then rose again and introduced the morning's topic with these words:

> Our topic is the issue of economic justice. The agenda committee felt it was important to frame a question with the focus on practical/moral/spiritual, which we hope will inspire us. This is it: "How can we renew our commitment to our testimonies of truth, justice and equality and discern action to take our witness forward?"
>
> We have asked two speakers to introduce their own reflections on this question. We will then have a time for Friends to share our responses. We may then need to draft a minute which reflects where we have got to.
>
> I will ask the speakers to begin when they feel ready.

Each speaker then stood and addressed the assembly: the first, to speak about the work of Quaker Peace & Social Witness (QPSW) with the ethical trading initiative; the second, to describe the faith in action of homelessness projects undertaken by Quaker Social Action (QSA). There was quiet, then a brief break. On re-assembling, the clerk then invited contributions.

Over the next thirty minutes, the clerk called nine Friends to speak. Each time she raised her head, some ten or twelve standing figures could be seen across the rows of seated people, waiting for their turn. Those who were not called sat again, while one spoke. Some did not stand more than once. Others stood and waited their turn, sat down, and again, when the next speaker had finished, rose to their feet.

From my notes at the time, this list gives a sense of what each speaker had to say. The third of these is a verbatim transcript of all that that Friend stood to say (with evident emotion). The rest are the opening words only of what in each case was a contribution lasting a few minutes:

1. I was just wondering if people know about Emmaus, the charity for homeless people…
2. There is a problem of large organisations…
3. We should not have the choice to torture and enslave.
4. I live on a housing estate, some of the poorest in Europe…
5. There is a concentration of power that makes truth a casualty…
6. The global economic system is committed to the idea of growth…
7. We are talking of getting out of comfort zones; let us get out of the comfort zone of the BBC…
8. I am grateful for the session. QPSW is supporting Friends by doing what they do…
9. There's no peace without justice. We struggle for people in health care to get basic support and benefits…

Twelve people (including myself) were standing, possibly more, also hoping to be called to speak. The clerk looked up once again and said that she would take one more contribution and then draft a minute. This is my note of that contribution, made by another Friend:

> I feel that we need to go back to a place of prayer, and… I belong to a generation who, during the long struggle against apartheid in South Africa, for months and years agreed to hold those people in the Light at 9 o'clock every night…

Discipline and upholding

The meeting was then silent.

Capturing the minute

The clerks bowed over the table together, working on the minute, drawing on these ten contributions. The assembled Friends were still. After a few minutes, the clerk rose to her feet, stood holding her large notebook and read out the draft. She then sat down again.

During the next fifteen minutes, some half a dozen Friends from different parts of the gathering stood waiting to be called, to offer still more amendments. One by one, the clerk called three to speak and they offered amendments as follows:

> (First speaker): I am very grateful for that minute, which has captured much. However, there is one word in the first sentence which I think is a mistake. You talk of testimonies *of*, but I think it should be testimonies *to*.

> (Second speaker): I just wonder, shouldn't we have the word "integrity" in there?

> (Third speaker): I think the minute has got one thing wrong. There is no economic system that has been created in one go. I would suggest the wording "global economic system" is changed to "legal framework of economic activity".

After conferring with the assistant clerk, the clerk rose and answered the third speaker first: "We feel that 'global economic system' was the term used this morning, so we are minded to keep it." She went on to accept the first correction, noted a deletion that the clerks themselves wanted to make ("doing much in small ways") and then, looking up, asked: "With those changes, is that minute now acceptable?" One more participant stood and pressed for the word "integrity", and asked for some wording that would also express a recognition of the needs of the unemployed. At this point, the clerk stood, said that the clerks would add "integrity" and then told the gathering:

> We wonder if, as it is not a verbatim minute, the minute would now serve as it is without further additions. I can see Friends needing to be released to collect children. Are we in a position to accept? (murmurs of "I hope so")

The full accepted minute (see Appendix 1) was the result of a time in which several hundred people worshipped together and arrived at a statement around which they were willing to unite. It was a minute of "exercise", intended to give expression to the sense of the meeting, on that topic, at that time. The clerks at the table were there to do more than record a decision. Their purpose was to capture and convey a collected voice and spirit – both the work of making the decision and the decision itself.

Teaching the discipline

In terms of setting out the discipline, I noted two requests that the clerk made of the meeting. First, she asked for speakers to be brief, pointing out this had not been happening, reminding Friends of the equal opportunity for speaking that this would give to others:

> I would ask that in offering responses, Friends will strive to be concise. This was not always the case at our meeting yesterday. We need to allow time between contributions. It would be helpful if we could show courtesy to the meeting, to enable as many as possible to minister.

The second request to Friends was made after the break, when the meeting was resuming. This time, she asked the meeting to remember to listen, and to check if what they thought they wanted to say was really needed. She said:

> After each spoken contribution, the clerks are reflecting on what has been said. We would ask you to do the same, and if you feel you have a message, be asking yourself whether you still have it. When clerks look up, we do ask Friends to test

your leadings, and if you are sure it is for the meeting, please keep it concise."

The combination of these two messages was to say to the hundreds of us seated in the tent: "Watch the clerks; see what we are doing; do it, too." And: "Think hard whether what you want to say really needs saying. If it does, then keep it short."

Only now, rereading this, do I see my own experience of "upholding" (which I described earlier) for what it was. Together, the clerk and the gathered meeting had been teaching. I, in my turn, had been learning.

Small

At the time of my visit there in September 2011, Milford Haven was one of fourteen local meetings in South Wales Area Quaker Meeting. Here is something from my notes about the background to the meeting for worship for business that I joined:

> Seven Friends and I are seated in a semi-circle of chairs and benches facing the clerk, sitting at a table with papers in front of her. At the clerk's invitation, we begin with a few moments' worship.
>
> This year, Milford Haven Quakers are celebrating the 200th anniversary of the opening of their meeting house. Not one of the current members and attenders actually lives in Milford Haven. Most, like the clerk, seem to have between five and ten miles' journey by car to get to meeting. Public transport is sparse on Sundays.
>
> Numerically, it is a very small meeting, with a majority aged over sixty. The attendance of eleven Friends at the 11am meeting for worship this Sunday morning is a little higher than usual, with eight (including the clerk) returning to the meeting room for their monthly meeting for worship for business after the coffee break.

Small it may be, but this is a busy period for the meeting community, who are using the anniversary as an opportunity to promote current Quaker life as well as its part in local history. The agenda for this morning's meeting includes planning for four Saturday events within the meeting house in September alone: area meeting the following week; opening of a two-week "Creative Quakers" exhibition the next day; a history "tea party" on the Saturday after that and a local poetry society visit a week later.

This is my record of what followed, grouped into the two aspects of the meeting's activity that I observed: living the discipline and making the decisions.

Living the discipline

The clerk, Jean Lewis, looked up and gave out paper copies of this meeting's agenda and the minutes of the previous meeting. She then said: "Please be tender with me as we do not have J today to write the minutes" and went on to tell the meeting: "I have circulated the minutes of the last meeting and I shall now sign them" (the copy kept in the minute book).

The agenda had eight items. At the third, "premises", the meeting welcomed the completion of a new gate. M said he would insert some new washers that were needed for the bolts. The clerk asked if the meeting thought it would be appropriate to send a letter of appreciation to R, who had hung the gate. Several murmurs or nods of agreement followed. She said, "So I will minute that: 'Clerk to write to R thanking him for the gate'."

Another Friend, A, noted that the neighbours of the meeting house had shown appreciation of the newly painted wall, as well as the gate. She added: "They also said that the graffiti people will be here soon".

In a rueful aside, the clerk said: "I won't minute that."

The meeting went on to discuss arrangements for the area meeting on the following Saturday, to be held at this meeting house. First, the domestic matters. (Who will bring the milk? What kind of refreshments? We'll need savoury things – a lot of people have

Discipline and upholding

a long journey back. I'll bring quiche. The usual Indian savouries? Sandwiches? What sort? What quantities? We usually get twenty-five to thirty people. K and A agreed to do enough for fifteen each.)

Making the decisions

Next came a discussion on the programme for the day. The clerk began by saying, "Here is a tentative minute: 'R is organising the day. It's on the theme of diaries'". Another Friend modified this, adding: "And then we'll do some bulb-planting in the garden". The clerk read out her amended minute ("R is organising the nurture. It will begin with bulb-planting. Then a presentation.") and added: "We'll need some trowels". There was some more discussion in the group about timing and an extra activity in the afternoon. The clerk read the minute as it had now developed:

> There will be a presentation about Ab's diary in the morning. The bulb-planting in the garden will start in the afternoon followed by a creative activity. All who can, have been asked to bring a trowel.

"Are we happy with that?", she asked. "Yes" was the murmur, one Friend adding, with a smile: "And if it's torrential rain and a thunderstorm we'll just have to plant on a different occasion."

At this stage, some conversation began about the issue of what to do with any money taken at the exhibition. (At the same time, one Friend had to leave the room to speak to a visitor to the meeting house, visible outside the door. She returned to say: "That was the chap from the museum, wanting copies of our walks leaflet as they have run out of them.") The clerk reminded the meeting that they were still on item 8, "September planning". One Friend suggested that any money taken from the exhibition could be used for a meeting house fund – maybe calling it the "bicentenary fund". The clerk then offered these words as a possible draft minute:

> We agree that money from ticket sales, recipe books, also donations should form a "bicentenary fund".

At this, A said: "We did also say 'sales of any crafts', if Friends are willing."

The clerk responded: "So I've added that. And we can decide later what we will use it for? 'Use of which will be decided later'. Do you want me to read that again?" (Yes). She then read out the whole minute.

There followed a couple of exchanges about a marquee and some tables, after which the clerk simply said: "I'm not going to minute this. All I'm going to minute is: 'Arts and Crafts exhibition. We have discussed arrangements'. Further questions were raised: Should there be complimentary tickets for meeting house neighbours? What costumes could be found for those Friends doing the welcoming? What food would it be appropriate to offer? What kind of period games could be offered for the children? After a few minutes, the clerk asked: "Should I simply say 'The arrangements are ongoing'?" (Meeting: yes). After a couple more brief items, the clerk invited the meeting to end with a few minutes' silence.

Having begun at 12.15, the meeting ended at 1.30pm. From then until I had to set off to catch my train, I stayed on with four Friends who were getting tables and display boards out for the exhibition. We ate sandwiches together while the rain poured down outside.

As I thought about it later, this had been a meeting primarily working on the what, how and who of a set of larger decisions already made as to whether and when. The meeting had already committed itself to run these events. Small in number, those present would by and large be those who would carry out this commitment. So there was no delegation to be done. This was the best time to be discussing the quantity and content of the sandwiches, using the same respect for each other in considering it as they would if they were considering larger policy questions.

The Friends present had already worshipped in stillness together for forty-five minutes. In this, the meeting for business that followed, there were few intervals of silence. Of the seven Friends present, two remained almost completely silent; and two others provided most of the spoken contributions. During the meeting, the clerk did, or spoke of doing, three kinds of writing, all signifying decisions being made and/or concluded:

Discipline and upholding

- signing the previous meeting's minutes;
- drafting and checking a minute for each item in this meeting; and
- recording the meeting's instruction that she should write a thank-you letter to the gate-fixing man.

The one thing she also did several times, which would be striking to anyone not used to Quaker ways of doing business, was to check with the group about what she was writing or proposing to write. This is an active means of enabling the group to notice where they were getting to on the journey towards their decision and is the same kind of behaviour that the clerk of Yearly Meeting was using. Its message is:

> I, your clerk, am drafting this minute, but you, the meeting, are all responsible for the decision and its satisfactory record. Is this what you think? Is this how we want to proceed? Uphold me. Attend to our shared responsibility.

This clerk did it by saying: "So I'll minute that"; "I won't minute that"; "Here is a tentative minute"; "I will amend the draft minute"; and "Are we happy with that?"

While this clerk did not give a formal reminder of discipline, what she did do – as Lis Burch had done at the Yearly Meeting session – was keep Friends' attention on it. As I sat there, I felt: this, too, is the work of discernment, with the Spirit involved. The only minute that she read back in full to the meeting before asking for acceptance was the one concerning money raised at the exhibition – possibly because it was a longer minute with an amendment and one that carried an extra responsibility.

Afterword

The idea in Quaker business meetings is that participants should be active: listening, listening and listening again. In the throng of Yearly Meeting, it was impossible for the body of the meeting to do anything other than wait for the clerk to call individuals to contribute. In practical terms, the sheer numbers present meant that any individual waiting to speak would only be heard once the clerk had asked the nearest steward to give them a microphone.

In the intimacy of the smaller meeting, the situation was different. Each individual had things to say. They were sitting close together and could hear each other speak. There were a couple of moments when two people spoke at the same time so that – with the distraction of a visitor seen through the open door – the discipline loosened and for a few minutes two conversations were going on at once.

For any Friend seeking to know Quaker ways of doing business, first-hand experience of local or area meetings is essential, and of Yearly Meeting highly desirable. However, as we saw from the vignettes in the previous chapter, any meeting varies from one session to the next: disciplines weaken, Friends seem to "go off the point", the promised silent moments seem few and far between, and the whole thing feels disappointing. There can be a tension between the informality of a group of people who know each other well and the more formal behaviour expected from the disciplines.

Participation in the theatre of a yearly meeting in session, by contrast, can feel awe-inspiring. We witness what almost seems like a performance by the clerk, holding the meeting together, presenting back to us our words and more. The use of microphones for speakers from the floor adds to the dramatic effect. It seems a long way indeed from providing us with a model for our own small business meetings, with matters of catering and painting of gates to consider.

Reviewing Barry Morley's three components for arriving at the sense of the meeting (release, a long focus, and transition to Light), I found these seemed to offer a helpful lens through which to consider the ten ministries at the Yearly Meeting session – and the drafting of the minute that followed. But within the business of the smaller meeting, these stages were less visible.

As to Patricia Loring's idea of "clerking together", I think we could say this took place, to some degree, in both sessions. In the larger meeting, the acceptance of the discipline, the responses offered to the first draft, and – perhaps most of all – the silent waiting and listening of the large majority of the meeting all played an important part in the process. In the small meeting, we see a clerk who quite simply asks for upholding at the start and, despite some raggedness about the discipline, receives an attentive acceptance of the agenda sequence. Between them, all present were contributing something towards the decisions that had to be found – not to mention the delegation of who would implement them.

Chapter 4 will look in more detail at this clerkly role, and in Chapter 5 there will be more on the process of moving from draft to completed minute, with amendments offered by those in the meeting. First, I will explore further what is going on during the process of discernment. As the case study shows, it can sometimes take a good deal longer than one meeting to arrive at widespread unity on a matter.

CHAPTER 3:

Unity and discernment

So far, we have been considering the worship basis for Quaker decision-making, the discipline that comes with it, and some thoughts on upholding.

This chapter focuses on the process of decision-making itself, by which a meeting of Quakers sets about discovering and following a divine leading as to the decision it needs to make. The decision sought is something for which those present may not always feel agreement, and which is beyond both consensus and the wish of a majority. This is "unity", the subject of the first section; in the second we consider the process of corporate discernment that precedes it. Section three sets out the story of this process on a single issue, in a series of stages, over a period of time, during which the exercise of disagreement and difference sometimes took the form of "threshing".

Unity

In order to make decisions, Quakers aspire to find unity with the help of a two-layered discipline and gathered discernment. For true unity to be found, each one present has to feel that they have been listened to; for in the last resort, it depends on

> a willingness to recognise and accept the sense of the meeting as recorded in the minute, *knowing that our dissenting views have been heard and considered* (Qf&p 3.06; my emphasis).

In a meeting for worship for business, the Quaker emphasis on direct access to God means that each one present is attending to the divine within themselves and in the room. The resulting decisions, in Patricia Loring's words, do not express a unity of opinion but rather a feeling gained through a sense of oneness in God's presence, sometimes called "group mysticism". The accepted minute recording the discerned decision is, then, an expression of "the unity and peace of the meeting" (Loring 1997, p. 85).

In the previous chapter, I gave the example of my own experience of this sense of unity at the 2011 Yearly Meeting Gathering. This second example, from another Yearly Meeting, is one that Floe Shakespeare gave me:

> It was the Britain Yearly Meeting in session at York, and the topic before us was same-sex marriage. I was out of kilter with the whole thing. I don't agree with marriage. I am a lesbian. I had come with a women's group and I'd spent the week arguing with my mates. So I went to the final session out of key with what seemed to be emerging. But what happened in the course of the drafting process, without me having to say or do anything, was a minute which expressed all of us. It was a magic moment. I somehow felt – I am a part of this.
>
> At a later meeting (of Quaker Lesbian Gathering) I had the same sense of something decided that was right for the group, even though it was not right for me. I know it was the knowledge that everybody had been listened to that gave me that feeling.

As in my own experience, despite misgivings and resistance, Floe found herself able to submit to a group discernment: a process, as she put it to me, that calls for a "letting go of our egos". In so doing we had to put down, as it were, the baggage of our life experience outside Quaker business meetings.

Timothy Phillips put this well when he told me in a phone interview how he explained the idea of unity to non-Quakers:

> I say, what we are trying to achieve is unity. And we are trying to achieve it within limited time. There isn't endless time, for any of us. That's a reality to be acknowledged.
>
> Then I explain that the first thing we do is to start the meeting with a short period of reflective shared silence. We have come with busy heads, but we are here to seek unity, or (if you prefer) the will of God – so we need to park all that lot by the door. We may have come with preconceived ideas as to what needs deciding and what the decisions should be. We have to park those, too. Unity is about focusing on the issue: discerning through to a decision which is best for that issue, not what is best for our selfish interests.

Unity and discernment

As he sees it, it is by leaving personal agendas at the door that Quakers arrive at unity. However, decisions around which a group can unite sometimes need more time than one meeting can provide, and the discernment process may go through several stages. To arrive at full unity, its grounding in the Divine needs also to be full. This is the view of Felicity Kaal in one of three prize essays on "The future of Quakerism in Britain Yearly Meeting" in *Friends Quarterly* (May 2010). Like Peter Eccles and Christine Davis, she sees the need for Quakers to restate their faith in this, and in order to do so, "to teach the discernment process and… develop the spiritual muscle" (p. 70). For her, being a Quaker means accepting the reality of the "Spiritual Realm". Quakers, she says, need corporately to offer a new conception of God, to move on from defining themselves by who they are not; and to retrieve the meeting for worship for business and its basis in divine guidance. The social conditions of the past have gone, when Quakers were a tight-knit, cohesive community of "birthright" Friends who knew each other, knew the previous decisions and why they had been taken. Quakers must, she says, adapt accordingly.

In Chapter 2, we saw how in Barry Morley's view of the corporate discernment process, "release" may lead, via "long focus", to Light. Felicity Kaal offers a rather different sequence: a move from intellectual and rational work towards divine guidance. This guidance, she says, only becomes available after fully exhausting all other routes. Exercise intellects and creativity first; then the way will open for a leading:

> To have hearts and minds prepared is first to do all that the human mind, skills and ingenuity can do towards solving the problem or making the decision. All possible avenues must be explored and all possible actions taken. It is only when that is complete, when all our thoughts, ideas and feelings on the subject have been explored and laid to rest, that we are able to clear our minds and open to Divine guidance as to the right way forward (Kaal 2010, p. 78).

With contentious matters, it is important, she says, to provide a form – such as worship sharing or threshing – in which to gather and explore facts, put forward ideas, share experience and listen to each other. But for unity to be found, that is not all. At the final stage, "when rationality has taken us as far as it is able", participants in the meeting need to go into worship and listen for divine guidance, God's will or the Inward Light (p. 79).

Such a progression may take different periods of time, according to the decision to be taken. When the local meeting in the previous chapter was discerning what to do with the takings from the exhibition, they needed time, but not a long time. All those with an interest in the decision were present. There were no other causes competing for the income. They were familiar with their own organisation and its culture. And they were in a position of power, as well as responsibility, to take the decision there and then.

Other decisions, however, may need more than one meeting. Unity over several aspects may take a revisit. Unity among those not present at this meeting may need to be further discerned. There may be a need for a time to explore disagreement. In the search for unity, differences may emerge that need more time than is possible in one session. Too often, it is said, such differences may not be sufficiently heard, so that a true unity may feel out of reach.

Discernment

Patricia Loring's account of a two-year period of discernment in a meeting in New England is helpful here. The question was one of the heat in the meeting house; the context, a part of the country where "the quality of the summer air as well as its temperature are serious health issues", when those at meeting (in a room above a converted garage) poured with sweat and had swimming heads by mid-morning. From June to the end of September, elderly and infirm members stopped attending meeting altogether. Out of this context emerged the proposal to install air conditioning.

There were objections. There would clearly be harmful effects on the environment. There would also, it was felt, be something wrong in the meeting affording such a commodity so close to a neighbourhood where people lived in extreme poverty and had no choice but to endure the extreme heat without such relief. In addition, still other Friends felt that it was not only ecologically but spiritually sound to accept the heat as it was, to accept it as the natural consequence of life in this particular climatic zone (Loring 1997, p. 161).

For two years the matter went to and fro – or, in Quaker terms, "was before the meeting" – with strong feelings and no resolution. They tried other technical solutions that cost less than the full air conditioning system, but they did not work. "Adversarial feelings" were emerging; Friends were at odds with each other, pressing their own positions. Finally, when the whole topic was completely stuck, one Friend stood up and spoke of her distress at this situation. She told the meeting that

> if we could not find our way to loving unity, she would never again be comfortable with us in a demonstration or in a letter-writing exercise advising distant people, divided by historic conflicts ... to settle their differences and live in peace (Loring 1997, p. 161).

There was a long silence. At length, one by one, those who had opposed the air conditioning spoke, writes Loring, not to unite with the feeling about air conditioning being right, but to "set aside the differences that stood in the way of unity". The meeting went ahead with air conditioning. It also went on to make a new commitment: to support a low-cost housing development locally and to explore further ways "of being more useful to homeless people" (Loring 1997, pp. 161–62).

Patricia Loring offers this story of reaching unity as an example of a meeting getting beyond strong opinions to arrive at a solution that enables a full answer to the meeting's problem: one that would both enable a renewed attendance at meeting and meet its concern to give support to the community beyond it. Of course, in deciding to go ahead with the air conditioning, Friends also had to accept their responsibility for the environmental impact this extra use of energy would cause.

Discernment, in the view of Roy Payne, is a measured matter, and difference can produce growth. Between July and November 2010 he was one of several contributors to a lively correspondence on the subject of the "Quaker business method" in the letters pages of *The Friend*. On the question of dissent, he wrote, experienced Friends may stand and say that they cannot agree with an emerging decision, but do not then attempt to block the discernment; for they know that what they are seeking is not uniformity, or unanimity for that matter, but unity – with the meeting united in accepting that "this is the right minute for this particular meeting at this particular time". Rightly used, Roy Payne writes, lack of unanimity can be a growing point for the meeting concerned (10 September, p. 9).

The Quaker practice of listening in silence to varieties of spoken ministry in meetings for worship is relevant here. The key guidance on such ministry found in *Quaker faith & practice* 3.10 can be summed up like this: "Do not minister more than once; do not minister for too long; and try to make sure that the ministry is for the meeting, not merely for yourself." In practice, such ministry may be short or long, with elders responsible for reminding Friends, as necessary, of the discipline; Ben Pink Dandelion reports one survey that found that vocal ministries may last for anything from half a minute to ten minutes (Pink Dandelion 2004, p. 99). A spoken ministry may tax listeners not only because it is long, but also for other reasons. Quaker advice on this is firm:

> Receive the vocal ministry of others in a tender and creative spirit. Reach for the meaning deep within it, recognising that even if it is not God's word for you, it may be so for others (*Advices & queries* 12, in *Qf&p* 1.02).

More than one Friend has suggested to me that this practice during meeting for worship develops a useful capacity to listen thoughtfully in business meetings, resisting irritation, impatience and/or the impulse to jump up and disagree.

The discipline of receiving ministry can provide the basis for spiritual growth: Alison Leonard tells a story reflecting on this. For some weeks, she had felt a growing frustration at having to listen to what she felt was a "parsonical", preachy kind of ministry by another

Friend in her meeting. After yet another of these, she made up her mind to go to the meeting's elders and ask them to speak to the Friend concerned.

> I'd put a stop to this, I thought. He was upsetting a lot of people besides me. Yes, he'd probably be hurt – but too bad, he should be made to realise the harmful effect he was having. I resolved to act soon, knowing that I was right.
>
> I was getting dressed one morning when the revelation came. It came to me from some deep inner source that this man had as much right to express his spiritual insights in his own words as I had. I knew how I would feel if I was told to be silent because what my spirit said – or, if you like, what the Spirit said through me – was judged unacceptable to the ears of others. That judgement had been delivered to me for years in the very structure of the churches where I'd struggled to be a faithful member. Was I now going to say it to someone else? (Leonard 1995, p. 83)

This is a moment of personal rather than group discernment, but it has a similar quality to the transitions that Barry Morley and Felicity Kaal suggest. Alison Leonard had allowed herself to shift from the close focus to a longer one; to open herself to move from a rational position of right/wrong to a spiritual self-questioning. Such a shift allows for the certainty of an individual or group being right to give place to the possibility that they "may be mistaken" (*Advices & queries* 17). This is listening to what has been heard not just once (live, as it were) but a second time (to its recording in the memory), allowing the faith in essential goodness to enter into the reflection.

Discernment can be seen as a process not only of finding a decision, but of taking responsibility. This is a view that Lizz Roe offered at a weekend course on the subject held at Woodbrooke Quaker Study Centre, which I attended in September 2011. She described the stages of a meeting's discernment process as beginning before the business meeting itself, with *awareness* and *exploration* of a possible topic for inclusion on the agenda. Friends may then seek clerks' help in bringing this to the meeting (in so doing, inviting others to become aware and explore the issue further). With *inspiration* or guidance of the Spirit, discernment may lead to unity as to what needs doing next. With this unity comes a sense of *ownership* and an *undertaking* to move to the next step. To help us recall this list of stages, Lizz pointed out to us that, happily, they correspond to the vowel letters: A, E, I, O, U.

Threshing meetings

A particular tool for resolving difference or disagreement can be what Quakers call "threshing meetings". The idea is to provide an opportunity to fully voice views and feelings outside the framework of discernment. This is the guidance in *Quaker faith & practice*:

> This term currently denotes a meeting at which a variety of different, and sometimes controversial, opinions can be openly, and sometimes forcefully, expressed, often in order to defuse a situation before a later meeting for worship for business. Originally, the term was used to describe large and noisy meetings for convincement of "the world's people" in order to "thresh" them away from the world (*Qf&p* 12.26).

The leaflet of the same title (published 2011, available at www.quaker.org.uk) provides guidance and practical help on how best to use such meetings. There are four circumstances, it says, in which Friends might consider organising a threshing meeting:

- Where a difference of opinion(s) is causing distress or disturbance to individuals or the meeting, or delaying a necessary decision.
- Where a potentially contentious or controversial issue needs to be addressed.
- To allow views to be expressed to enable movement towards greater clarity.
- As a preliminary to a decision-making meeting.

Unity and discernment

For three of these cases, it seems clear that Quakers regard threshing as a useful process in its own right, as well as being one that may release a meeting to go on and discern unity on a topic.

In a national organisation such as Quakers in Britain, discernment on one occasion and in one place may lead to a ripple effect, as the following account suggests.

Discernment: a case study

In this story, the sequence of discernment shows a series of stages over a period of nearly a year: a process that will continue as other Friends come to learn of the minuted outcome of the "key" discernment. It was a process that engaged all area meetings in Britain Yearly Meeting, together with the national body that supports Yearly Meeting between its gatherings: Meeting for Sufferings (often referred to as "Sufferings"). The topic at issue came up three times at Sufferings, resulting in three different written minutes. The accounts that follow draw from those minutes, from interviews with two Friends who took part, and from the notes sent in for this project by clerks from area meetings that considered the matter in between. As we will see, at least one of these AMs found it helpful to thresh their ideas in order to deal with the issue they were facing.

Boycott, divestment and sanctions (BDS)

The issue of the non-violent strategies to end the long conflict in Israel-Palestine has exercised Quakers for a long time, and particularly since the establishment in 2001 of the British branch of the Ecumenical Accompaniment Programme in Palestine and Israel (see www.quaker.org.uk/eappi). The separation barrier encroaching on Palestinian land, the demolitions of Palestinian homes, a system of permits that persistently restricts Palestinian freedom of movement, and above all the continued building of Israeli-only housing developments (known as "settlements") all over Palestinian land has led to an international concern. Peace efforts remain stuck. Humanitarian law and human rights continue to be flouted. There was a call for a campaign of boycott, divestment and sanctions. During December 2010 British

Quakers considered a response to this.

Early that year, Quaker Council for European Affairs (QCEA) had been considering reports from the work of Quaker Peace & Social Witness and exploring the recommendations made by a 2009 report from Christian Palestinians sent to churches in the world community (Kairos Palestine, 2009). QCEA sent a summary of its work and the call for solidarity from the Palestinian churches to Meeting for Sufferings.

December to February

The December meeting received these reports and agreed they should be read and considered further. There was a bare minute of record noting receipt of them and asking Quakers in local and area meetings to reflect on their recommendations – and, by implication, for this meeting to come back to the topic in light of this reflection.

At its next meeting, Sufferings duly did this. This is how its clerk, Christine Cannon, recalled the experience some months later:

> The item on BDS was on the agenda. I had been ill before, so I had not been able to join the pre-meeting. This was my first meeting as clerk. Someone popped up and started off straight away. We had only allocated it an hour.
>
> There was criticism afterwards. Several Friends came up to me and told me very firmly it had not been balanced, that they had stood several times and not been called, it had not been right. Should I have given it more time? (Interview, 2 August 2011)

The minute that the meeting accepted was inconclusive. In terms of action, it "encouraged" Friends to study the subject of boycott and "asked them to consider further what action may be possible". Patricia Cockrell was one of those who felt unhappy with this and with the process and lack of time:

> Marigold Bentley [Assistant General Secretary of QPSW

Unity and discernment

and also Secretary of the Quaker Committee for Christian & Interfaith Relations] had introduced her paper in a very Quakerly way.

She was careful not to lead the meeting to one view or another. It was a very good and even-handed introduction. So when others began to speak, I was waiting for someone to stand up to say, "Yes, but look where the power is". Instead, people began to talk about other things. One Friend stood up and spoke about the eschatology of the Kairos document at some length. Another Friend spoke at length about Holocaust Memorial Day. I felt the clerk could not intervene, because the Friend concerned was in such a deep place. Others also ministered. I stood again. This time I wanted to say, yes, that pain is real. But today there is pain within another community. I wanted to bring it back to now. Again, I was not called.

Just six weeks earlier, Patricia had completed a three-month term serving as an Ecumenical Accompanier in the West Bank and felt that much had been left out. Not being called to speak, despite standing up several times, had been frustrating.

February to April

After the meeting, Christine Cannon sent out the minutes, together with her usual follow-up letter. Many area meetings had the issue on their next agenda. For example, as Katie Evans reported, West Wiltshire and East Somerset AM engaged in "a substantial period of discernment" on the topic, "with silences between contributions". Amendments offered by participants meant that the draft minute presented by the clerks was re-drafted three times before acceptance.

Meanwhile, in North Cumbria AM, Friends heard the report from their representative, and some seven or eight Friends stood to offer contributions. In her report on this, Kath Worrall said:

> Within our AM we have a former Ecumenical Accompanier who has given a number of talks. As a result local Ffriends

have heard a first-hand account of this subject and … the ministry was measured and concerned.

Eventually, their meeting arrived at the following minute:

Boycott, Divestment, Sanctions and Israel-Palestine

We have heard a report from our representative on Meeting for Sufferings of the difficulties concerning the Israel/Palestine situation and the call for boycott, divestment and sanctions. We realise that this is an important, possibly even the most important, issue facing the world today.

We hope that Meeting for Sufferings will continue to engage with this and try to find a way forward for Britain Yearly Meeting. We believe that Friends should work for guidance individually and act as they are led. We ask our clerk to forward this to the clerk of Meeting for Sufferings.

As Kath Worrall commented, for this meeting it felt clear that

views differ and there is no single response that is wholly appropriate. Hence the need to "work for guidance individually and act as led".

All around the country, AMs arrived at their own discernments on this topic. In all, fourteen area meetings, including these two, composed and sent their own minutes to the clerks of Meeting for Sufferings; and the Sufferings clerks in their turn decided to bring the matter forward to the next meeting, in April.

At that meeting, the assistant clerk presented to Sufferings a summary of the fourteen minutes. As Patricia Cockrell recalled,

The clerk opened the item by saying "There has been a lot of interest in this matter. I hope that we can keep our consideration to the twenty-first century. I would like to ask any Friends with knowledge of Israeli organisations and personal experience in the area to offer any information they may have."

This was subtle guidance: acknowledging the deep horror of the Holocaust voiced in the February meeting, reminding the meeting of the other kind of persecution represented by the current conflict, and recognising there were those in the meeting who had something to contribute about Jewish calls for peace in Israel. Patricia went on:

> So I spoke. I made it personal. How I had met Israeli people and worked with Israeli and Palestinian human rights groups. I gave a list of some of the peace organisations and their activities.
>
> I spoke for a good seven minutes, I should think. And then I sat down. The clerks kept their heads down.
>
> They called no-one to speak for a full minute.

In arriving at the accepted minute, the meeting seemed to feel that it needed to fully set out the discernment not only of this meeting but also of the one held in February. The agreed minute (see Appendix 2) begins with a careful recognition that "a just peace for Palestine means security for Israel too" and that there had been nine years of Quakers witnessing in the region. It goes on to record what had emerged during the discernment, namely that the meeting considered whether or not to add nonviolent action to this witnessing, not "as punishment or revenge, but as an external pressure to achieve change".

Then comes a reminder of the commitment of early Quakers to a sense of connection with peoples of other faiths, and a note that the request for boycott comes "from those who will suffer most" (the Israeli peace groups as well as the Palestinians themselves). The decision to do it, the minute goes on, "would give hope to Palestinians and support to those in Israel who are working for peace". This, then, is the "call to action":

> We are clear then that it would be wrong to support the illegal settlements by purchasing their goods. We therefore ask Friends (Quakers) throughout Britain Yearly Meeting to boycott settlement goods, until such time as the occupation is ended.

The minute then listed further commitments:

- to continue dialogue with Palestinians and Israelis working for peace
- to act publicly by boycotting settlement goods
- to be well informed so that we can explain our decision
- not at this time to boycott Israel
- to pray for Israelis and Palestinians
- to treat tenderly those Friends who may find the boycott decision difficult.

Looking back on both meetings, Christine Cannon later told me:

> In response to the criticisms of the February meeting, and the minute we came to then, I think I would say: that's as far as we were able to go – and I couldn't promise at that stage that it would be on the agenda for the next meeting, because we had not yet prepared that.
>
> When it came to the April meeting, and I stood up to start reading out the minute we had come to, I found it hard to start. I was nearly moved to tears.

After the April meeting, Christine wrote a letter to go out with the minutes of the meeting. In it, she reported that even while Sufferings was still in session, Friends House was receiving phone calls about the decision to boycott. She asked that Friends would read the minute in full, which, as she put it, "conveys the spiritual root of our discernment". "There can be no sense of triumph", she went on. "These decisions are tinged with regret and sadness" – a reminder that what had been discerned was more than a single decision.

Unity and discernment

So the Friends in Meeting for Sufferings had undergone a three-stage process of discernment, linked by the processes in between these meetings undertaken by local and area meetings. Bearing in mind that the topic of BDS was only one of the items on the agendas of the December, February and April meetings, this gives some insight into how complex the process of worshipful decision-making in Quaker life can be.

May to November

After April 2011, the BDS decision rippled out through the national Quaker community and beyond. Area meetings were alternately inspired, confused and, in some cases, shocked. A number of area and local meetings sent in more minutes on the subject, emphasising the desire to respect the feelings of the Jewish community, especially in Britain, to support peacemakers from both sides, and to acknowledge the hurt and suffering in both communities (see *The Friend*, 17 June 2011, p. 4).

For Kingston & Wandsworth AM, what grew out of the Sufferings discernment was a further process: another example of how discernment may take more than a single meeting and include threshing. As Gillian Ashmore recalled:

> After the February Sufferings meeting, we were approached by local orthodox Jews who had read about this in the *Jewish Chronicle* [18 Feb 2011: "Now Quakers consider a boycott"]. They were very upset and wanted to meet and discuss this with us. So we met and it was absolutely them talking to us. We held as contemplative a meeting as possible but felt rather overwhelmed. My role in that group was to explain the decision-making processes of Quakers, which I did, but I found them sceptical. We thought it might end there and asked if they felt it was worth meeting again; they said yes, so we agreed to do that.
>
> The main thing I think we learned from that first meeting was something about their feeling of how it is to be a Jew in

the UK. They spoke of the fear of attacks, going to Jewish schools and synagogue; of feeling unheard about how life is for Jews in Israel, never feeling secure (they gave us several statistics of how many had been killed in rocket attacks); and of how, if you're a Jew – wherever you are – Israel is your last resort. We were able to say, we have heard and learned of your fear.

Before the second meeting, we had a pre-meeting, because we felt we had to consider "How are we going to handle this? We cannot stay silent again. We must find a way to say something".

This second meeting began in difficulty, repeating some of what had been said at the first one; but there was one in their group who seemed to assume leadership for them. He took a grip on things. Towards the end, we asked them what they wanted us to do, and their answer took us a little by surprise. It was: "We would like you to encourage the moderate Palestinian voice". We said we didn't know how we may do this, but we would try.

Once again, the Kingston & Wandsworth Friends needed to withdraw and voice feeling – this time, the sense of confusion and uncertainty. In Gillian's words:

We wondered what we were getting into and whether the meetings were serving a good purpose. Then there was an unexpected development. The Jews found out about an international organisation called One Voice, which runs training for both Palestinian and Israeli young people in giving them their voice. Their purpose is to help young people get across the message in their communities that peace is needed and possible and to mobilise support for negotiations to achieve a two-state solution. The young people set up meetings and get discussion going. They had two young people from Israel and Palestine about to do a speaking tour in the UK. The Jewish people did the work on this and suggested to us that they invite the organiser to meet with all of us.

At this third meeting, the One Voice organiser attended, and we agreed to ask the two young speakers to come and talk to us. The Jewish people in the meeting went away and set this up. They had proposed it could be a public meeting. But One Voice said no, that the two young people would be at the end of their tour and would be tired and nervous.

This fourth meeting, with these two speakers – one Israeli and one Palestinian – took place in Kingston at the beginning of November. At the time of writing, the Kingston dialogue group continues, despite some strong disagreements. Links with other peace-seeking organisations have been made and, as Gillian put it, "we have had some really good meetings". The group hopes to make a joint trip to Israel-Palestine.

There are to me two striking features of these experiences. First, Christine Cannon's declaration to other Friends about the minute discerned at the April Meeting for Sufferings: "There can be no sense of triumph". The process of discernment, captured in the minute, had been more than a "call to action". It was a recognition of the suffering caused by the violent conflict and what it raised for different groups.

Secondly, it was clearly valuable – as a preparation for peaceful dialogue – for Kingston & Wandsworth Quakers to take the time to thresh out their own feelings and ideas at their pre-meetings. They had taken the opportunity to listen to both this distress of a local community and to that among their own group, and follow their leadings stage by stage as to what might be done about it.

Afterword

If the purpose of business meetings is to "discern God's will", then there is a need for active upholding. The authors of *Practicing discernment together: finding God's way forward in decision making* call this "supportive prayer during decision making". For this, tentatively, they suggest three approaches:

> Perhaps the continuous prayer might be "thy will be done" or "we trust you" as we take our breaths. Perhaps it is the prayer of beaming God's love to all the participants. Perhaps it is holding a mental image of Jesus in the midst of the meeting.

Given the discipline of speaking rarely in meetings for worship for business, there are, as they point out, "plenty of opportunities to pray", for "while we listen attentively to others speak, we can simultaneously listen to God" (Fendall, Wood and Bishop 2007, p. 40).

For Quakers, praying assumes silence and listening as primary. Those Quakers who are "unprogrammed" in their forms of worship – that is, who worship silently, without prepared scripts or hymns – perhaps give that silence more emphasis than those who prefer a structured meeting. In his book *Encounter with silence* (1987) John Punshon gives an account of his first experience of this form of worship, and how it became the source of his religious development for the years that followed. In Quaker business meetings, he places importance in this worshipful use of silence, for as he puts it:

> The business meeting is a meeting for worship, and it takes place on the basis of silence just like any other meeting... Without the discipline of silent waiting, it would be impossible for the process to carry the theological weight Friends claim for it (Punshon 1987, p. 96).

From this sense of worship, when the meeting has ensured this "basis of silence", Linda Murgatroyd suggests (in a companion *Friends Quarterly* essay to Felicity Kaal's) that Quakers may come away from discernment with something else:

> I have often been amazed at the lightness of spirit in which I have left a Quaker business meeting, even though the meeting itself was hard work and the subject matter not of great personal interest. Joining in the work of discernment

often feels like a great privilege (*Friends Quarterly* May 2010, p. 10).

This chapter has considered how the process of discernment may entail different stages and various kinds of intensity, and how, given certain discipline, its worshipful purpose may be experienced. Most agenda items in local meetings for worship for business concern singular decisions about matters that seem apparently much more mundane than this. As I will describe in Chapter 6, these too can offer opportunities for loving discernment. Meanwhile, for such discernment to flourish, the business meeting also calls for well-supported clerking.

CHAPTER 4:

Clerks and clerking

Clerks and clerking

Until now, I have been considering the whole meeting at work. In this chapter, the focus is on clerks: on those "at the table". In terms of making a decision, it is the clerks, as the Quaker guidance has it, who are asked to watch how the thinking is going and choose the moment to help it to move on:

> The meeting places upon its clerk a responsibility for spiritual discernment so that he or she may watch the growth of the meeting toward unity and judge the right time to submit the minute, which in its first form may serve to clear the mind of the meeting about the issues which really need its decision (*Qf&p* 3.07).

Watch, judge and submit: that's quite a lot of responsibility – the clerk as both chair and secretary, observer and scribe. However, as the guidance points out, an important first use of a draft minute is to enable everyone there to discover what the decision is that they are in the process of making. As I will also be stressing in the next two chapters, the minute being submitted is only a draft; and the clerk is not alone.

As I said in the introduction, my first curiosity about Quakers grew from a desire to understand this process. Having come upon an organisation that supports the "minutes secretary" in such an unusual way, and having served as a clerk myself, I wanted to find out how other clerks experienced this approach. As the research developed, this curiosity grew to include the whole meeting's "responsibility for spiritual discernment", not only the clerk's.

In February and October 2011 I undertook two different surveys of clerking experience. The first was on general experiences of clerking. Fifty-six responses came back, from which I will look now at two particular themes that emerged:

- strategies and support for the writing side of the work; and
- spiritual aspects of the role as a whole.

Strategies and support

One focus in the questionnaire was on the clerkly task of drafting a minute during the meeting, while the rest of the meeting waits without speaking. To the question "what helps?", the overwhelming response was: silence, quiet and stillness. In Valerie James' words,

> Talking among themselves by those in the meeting is distinctly unhelpful and distracting.

If the clerk is on their own, they may call on Friends in the meeting who they know to have experience to help:

> If I am not sure, I call on the experience of past, very experienced clerks ("Nigel").

At the same time, no clerk is really on their own. Celia James had this message to any Friend new to clerking:

> Remember, it's not all up to you; the meeting is everyone.

Asking for help from a group of Quakers may result in more than you need; so, as she goes on to add, you could ask for another drafter to join you:

> Ask for help – if too much is given, ask one person to come forward and write a draft minute.

If the meeting is "everyone", if it works best, in Patricia Loring's phrase, when everyone clerks, then the idea of a clerk "asking for help" becomes a request made not from a sense of weakness, but from a position of collective strength: a reminder to the meeting of a shared responsibility. The work of minute-writing, however well-prepared, can be stressful:

> After each business meeting I breathe a sigh of relief that I've got away with it again! I'm not good at writing minutes, but

things do get recorded and things do get done, and no one's complaining (Angie Dunhill).

While the clerks draft a minute, they can be all too aware that they are keeping people waiting:

> I am very conscious of time, and people getting bored (Susan Bennet).

But there is a more confident view:

> My draft is a framework for their discernment (Trish Wickstead).

Maggie Norton's advice to a new clerk who might be getting stuck at the moment of trying to draft at the table encouraged a similar spirit: "It's not an examination. Say you're stuck. Someone will clarify." As a published poet and leader of writing workshops, Maggie evidently has a keen sense of the need to enable others to overcome their writing barriers. After a Woodbrooke clerks' training course she had attended in 2007, she wrote the poem "I think that I am hearing", about the business of clerking before and during the meeting. These lines offer an image of overcoming the struggle to draft:

> Overgrown shrubberies overwhelm
> but a fumbling first cut
> takes the brambles out.

Getting practice in doing this can help new clerks:

> I think writing Quaker minutes in the meeting can be hard at first, but it becomes easier with practice and with confidence. … If Friends generally helped each other with the business method in committees, it would be a good training ground for future LM/AM clerks (Ruth Heine).

The idea that the author of the Quaker minute, composed in session, is the meeting, not the clerk, is a message that seems to need repeating. To the new clerk who is getting stuck, Joycelin Dawes gives this advice:

> Be willing to take time. Try a minute and allow the meeting as a whole to exercise discernment in reflecting on it with you – the right phrase or way forward may be amongst them rather than in you.

"Remember", she adds, "that developing the draft with the meeting as a whole is an important part of the exercise of corporate discernment." The work of thinking feeds the work of composition – of writing; and in hearing the proposed writing read back, the meeting can discover what still needs to be said.

How does a clerk share the work? It can be a complex task to achieve the combination of reading the sense of the meeting, discerning an outcome and producing a rough draft of how the meeting might want to express that outcome. Many respondents to the question felt this is best undertaken when there are two clerks at the table – either working as co-clerks or as clerk and assistant clerk, as Heather Woolley had done:

> Usually the assistant clerk makes notes, leaving the clerk more able to focus on reading the sense of the meeting.

Suzanne Eade Roberts offered this pattern of sharing out the work:

> One person acts as chair of the meeting, calling different people to speak, and the other person makes notes and drafts minutes, and concentrates on listening to the spirit of the meeting.

> This lets one person be productive orally (i.e. speaking) and the other receptive (listening) then productive (writing).

In the Quaker context, Suzanne went on to explain, she feels this to

Clerks and clerking

be a more helpful distinction to make than the more common view of an active "chair" and a passive "secretary". Rather, as she put it:

> One person has responsibility for "managing" the meeting (raising each point on the agenda and calling people to speak) and the other for listening – to people and to God – putting down in words what s/he has discerned to be the sense of the meeting (and possibly, but not always, being the one to read this out as a draft minute).

In this arrangement of two clerks (whether described as clerk and assistant or co-clerks), one of the two is indeed an active and productive speaker. The other, while starting out as receptive, may then become productive too, in roughing out a first draft of the minute. It is a cycle of reception and production – and as the meeting hears and then contributes to this draft, there are more such cycles to come (see the next chapter). American Quakers routinely separate the roles into "presiding clerk" and "recording clerk". One guide gives a focus on the role of the first (Fendall, Wood and Bishop 2007); for the second, an article in *Friends Journal* (Philadelphia) looks at "The task of the recording clerk: spiritual exercise and ministry" (Hoover 2011).

Many stressed the need for clerks to give enough time for preparing for the meeting. Once at the table, they may then feel freer to do the listening and observing work and learn to trust the meeting to uphold them. Annette Candy, for example, felt it important to remind herself that she was "among friends". As she goes on to say, she also saw her task as one of encouraging (or upholding) others:

> Because I know local Friends, I find it easier to get the sense of the meeting … and can encourage people to take part who might not normally feel confident to speak – not by asking them directly, but by presenting questions/matters for consideration in a way that might make them less daunting to answer.

A spiritual role

The questionnaire did not include any specific questions about the spiritual aspect of the role, so the following three contributions were a bonus. In preparation for the meeting:

> I have some time for worship before writing the drafts for the meeting at home. I write one draft minute per page. There are big gaps so that I can make lots of changes if necessary (Caddi Ranyard).

From the experience of drafting during the meeting:

> I am ... surprised by some of the minutes that I have been able to write. I feel that we need to have confidence that we will be helped by the Spirit as well as by individuals to work for the meeting in this capacity (Fran Hewett).

In the same vein, Jo Poole offered this advice to any clerk feeling stuck at the drafting stage:

> Breathe deeply and open yourself to the Spirit. Do not try and do it alone, but accept the help given by the Divine.

For Jenni Brace, there can be a feeling of "everyone waiting on the Lord and upholding the clerk", and when this happens, the business meeting is as much a meeting for worship as the meeting for worship itself.

All but one of the respondents appeared to take it for granted that the management of the right ordering of a meeting for worship for business depended on the clerk's leadership. This returns us to the question raised in the first chapter: what role do elders play in this? Some elders clearly do intervene in some way:

> I remind people at the start that the clerks need silence to get a minute written – and it'll be quicker! We are supported by an appointed elder for each meeting for business. If anyone

Clerks and clerking

forgets, and speaks, it's the elder who does the reminding, not me (Zélie Gross).

"When it works well", wrote Valerie James,

> the Quaker business method is a very complete … way of conducting business … The role of the clerk is demanding, but also satisfying if the meeting has gone well and everyone has been able to unite in the decisions made.

I was glad to get this comment. *Quaker faith & practice* offers a vision of how it might feel for a clerk when the meeting as a whole is supported by "God's presence and help":

> In conducting the meeting and drafting minutes on its behalf, the clerk's abilities are strengthened by an awareness of being supported by the members of the meeting. Friends who have not known the unforeseen joy which comes from this experience may gain encouragement from this knowledge, should they be invited to serve. If the clerk's service is under concern in the certainty of God's presence and help in the meeting, then strength beyond her or his normal powers will be given (*Qf&p* 3.12).

Nominations

Quaker meetings cannot be understood without at least a summary of the process for finding and appointing people for the various roles. The job of nominations committees is to discern possible candidates for the role and ask if they would be willing to consider having their name put forward. If they are, the nominations committee convenor asks the current meeting clerk to put this on the agenda of the next business meeting, at which Friends discern the decision to appoint or not. All meeting roles are brought to the full meeting in the same way. When a Friend resigns from a role (or asks to be released), it is not a matter of asking someone else to volunteer. It is, rather, a case for the meeting to ask this committee to take on the task of seeking a successor (see *Qf&p* 3.22 and 3.23).

The role of clerk is generally seen to be not an easy one to fill. Things can begin to feel rather desperate. Rather than trying to find a single person to take on the responsibility alone, a solution can be co-clerking, in a pair or a team.

Co-clerking

Unlike the roles of elder or overseer (see *Qf&p* 12.10–12.18), Quaker guidance on the role of clerk is almost entirely framed in the singular. The *Quaker faith & practice* section on "Participation in meetings for church affairs" gives the following advice:

> Remember the onerous task laid upon *the clerk* and do all you can to assist (*Qf&p* 3.10; my emphasis).

While this is followed soon after by a reminder to "uphold *those at the table*", section 3.12 on clerkship begins by emphasising "the clerk":

> *The clerk* needs to have a spiritual capacity for discernment and sensitivity to the meeting. … *the clerk's* abilities are strengthened … *the clerk's* service (*Qf&p* 3.12; my emphasis).

It continues by defining the role of assistant clerk, there for consultation or as an apprentice, while the clerk "bears the final responsibility". But continuing in the same section, perhaps too easily skimmed over by the hasty reader, is a half-paragraph that offers an encouragement to break this focus on an individual, beginning with the words "Some meetings have found that co-clerkship can be highly successful".

What does "co-clerking" mean? Reference is made in the guidance passage to it being a means for two people to "complement each other" and (delightful phrase) provide a "lively and varied interpretation" of what clerks have to do.

Following another letter to *The Friend* (23 September 2011), asking readers to share their experiences of co-clerking, I received

Clerks and clerking

nineteen responses that gave a window on some patterns of co-clerking currently being explored. I asked two main questions:

- what division of labour did you have in that experience?
- what are your reflections on it?

Responses to my questionnaire stressed the unity of the partnership: "two clerks working as one, each being fully informed about all aspects of the work" and "sharing work according to each person's capabilities and availability". Co-clerking, another said, is useful when a meeting cannot find anyone to be a (single) clerk: it is

> a system that shares the duties of clerk to avoid one person being overloaded by the responsibilities of the office, e.g. when no-one in the meeting is willing or able to take on all the duties of clerk.

Of those who returned a completed questionnaire, most had a full three years' experience to draw on, and some had twice that. Most wrote about co-clerking in local meetings; some in area meetings. Among other meetings mentioned were: corporate elders and overseers group; area meeting trustees (finance and property committee) and the Quaker Disability Equality Group. One respondent attached a two-page guide on clerking used in "in-service training" for clerk teams in her local meeting.

Division of labour

From these responses, it is clear that although the two co-clerks may decide to divide up tasks in a certain way, these can often flow into each other as the working relationship develops. These were some of the ways of dividing up this work.

1. Alternating roles of facilitating and drafting within the meeting
In this arrangement, as one reply put it, one person reads (or leads) the meeting and the other drafts the minute, the two of them

checking over the minute together before the first presents it back to the meeting. Some took turns in this way from one agenda item to the next, in the same session, others from one meeting to the next.

2. Taking turns to "do" the whole meeting from one month to the next

This was an approach that Barbara Crawford evolved in two separate co-clerking experiences – with the proviso, she said, that the two clerks would always do the preparation for the business meetings together. From six years of co-clerking in York, Gill Bocock recalled sharing the work with her co-clerk "a month about, doing everything, but liaising about the actual business meeting". A variation on this approach was that of Jane Mutisya and Alex Tagg, who during their period of local meeting co-clerking took turns to "actually clerk the meeting", but "did everything else jointly".

3. Alternating the entire job for six months at a time

This means that each co-clerk is a clerk on their own each half year and sounds remarkably like single clerking – but in some meetings there is a third clerk (assistant or correspondence clerk) who provides a continuity, supporting first one, then the other.

4. "Facilitator" and "minutes clerk", working together the whole period

For Judith Eversley and Nicolas Francis, the working definition of co-clerking was simply "sharing the load". As co-clerks of an area meeting trustees finance and property committee, they found this to be the pattern of sharing in which they could best use their "complementary skills". It may be that there are other Friends who enjoy, as equals, an excellent clerk/assistant clerk relationship that could fit this model, without calling it co-clerking.

5. Co-clerks in a clerks' team

One solution can be a team. This was the arrangement reported from Uxbridge Quaker Meeting: one co-clerk with responsibility for local business meeting; a second for all correspondence, "acting as a post office"; a third reading all the notices at meeting. From Bradford-

Clerks and clerking

on-Avon Local Meeting, Ann Warren reported a team arrangement of seven: one acting as coordinating clerk; the other six working in pairs to prepare and clerk business meetings, with one usually acting as "chair", the other preparing and reading out the draft minutes. In Chester, Alison Leonard reported:

> Our Nominations Committee had come to the end of the trail where a single clerk/single assistant clerk was concerned. So they looked at new ways of clerking, heard that people were having a go with teams, and decided to ask around. They ended up with a team of four, and I'm one of the four.

This team divided up administrative roles and worked on a rota system of pairs to take turns with the eight business meetings in the year, alternating who would be clerk and who "assistant". Alison adds:

> We have regular team meetings to sort out the detail and to check how it's working. We always start our team meetings with a go-round to find out how we all are – our friendship matters a great deal, and eases the business.

Many respondents stressed the value of co-clerks giving time to look after each other in this way:

> It would only be worth doing if you wanted to and if you got on well with the other Friend (Barbara Crawford).

Looking at the pros and cons of the experience, respondents came up with almost entirely positive comments in two directions: benefits for the clerks and benefits for the meeting. This may, of course, be because only those who had had a good time chose to respond to my survey.

Benefits for the co-clerks

In terms of benefits, comments included: "neither of us had to carry the burden"; it "doesn't mean burdening one person with always being 'on tap'"; and it "avoids one person being overloaded". Two or three responses left it at that, but most wrote more. Diana Francis was clear:

> I just prefer co-clerking. It's good to concentrate on the minutes and let the other person facilitate, or vice versa, or take turns at being lead and backup in long meetings.

For her and her co-clerk Jan Arriens, the experience of nearly four years working together had been "flexible, efficient and fun". Gill Bocock enjoyed "the complete sharing and the (almost) lack of responsibility in alternate months". Jane Mutisya and Alex Tagg reflected that

> Neither of us would have had the confidence to do the job on our own, but sharing it made it possible. It was also a source of great personal enrichment working together on it. The whole experience not only drew us closer together personally but also gave both of us a new awareness of the spiritual dimension of Quaker meetings, and helped us to become clearer about what things we felt were important in the life of the meeting.

For Eleanor Tew, what was good about her co-clerking experiences (for her AM and for the Quaker Disability Equality Group) was that

> I feel able to use my gifts but generally do not have to take responsibility for what I would find most difficult. It is also good to be able to consult with my co-clerks.

Benefits for the meeting

Klaus Huber made an interesting point:

> The alternation of clerking and minute-taking meant that neither of us had to carry the burden of the entire clerk's job.

It also meant that the meeting wouldn't have to listen to the same voice all the time (my emphasis).

Quaker meetings for worship give a priority both to stillness and to the spoken word – and also to the use of reading aloud in meetings for worship for business (see the next chapter). Voices are the instruments of worship. To hear the same voice presenting items, guiding or reining in the discussion, and reading out draft minutes can be tiring for both speakers and listeners: variation may be helpful.

There is another benefit for the meeting in co-clerking. Eleanor Tew, for example, is clear on this. "I think co-clerking is better," she writes, "because it emphasises the notion of equality", enabling "a Friend who cannot carry out all aspects of the clerk's role because of disability to make a full and equal contribution."

For the meeting, the sense of more than one being at the table may promote or "model" this equality in an important sense:

> I think shared process management and ownership are fundamental to the feeling and reality of shared responsibility. It takes us outside of the "control" model and into a cooperative one in a highly symbolic and practical way (Diana Francis).

From over five years of co-clerking (with two different co-clerks) Marion Wells-Bruges also saw value for the meeting:

> It feels less hierarchical. Friends enjoyed seeing the two of us working together (my co-clerk is half my age). We could be light-hearted, supportive in moments of difficulty and take decisions that I would not care for a lone clerk to be doing.

The general agreement from all these responses is that it is good to share responsibilities. However, as Leslie Stevenson puts it, co-clerks need to establish "a good working relationship" if they are to avoid the risk of issues "falling between the cracks between two people, each not being sure what the other is doing/has done". Sandra Figgess suggests that it is worth co-clerks being aware of their different uses of email as a means of communicating. Otherwise, she says, there is a risk either that one may go ahead hastily on a decision, in the absence of a response from the other, or that both answer the same message.

In considering these findings, two observations occur to me:

1. Meetings go through change; they change size; members and attenders join or leave. Patterns of clerking may change, too.

This is through force of circumstance as much as choice. A meeting may move through three different clerking patterns in ten years: single clerk, clerks' team and a pair of co-clerks. Sue Bowers gives this example of another series of changes:

> In 2007, after having been a small twice-monthly weekday evening house group, our meeting set itself up as a new local meeting. ... We had only four Friends who were experienced enough to take on the role of clerk, two who had attended meetings before but were not involved in any roles, and the rest were new enquirers.

Over the next three years, their clerking patterns were: first, the house group convenor acting as clerk; then, four teams of clerk and assistant, each acting for three months of the year; and in the third year, two from these clerks, each with an assistant clerk, taking turns of six months each – along with one correspondence clerk throughout (to maintain continuity with Friends House).

2. Co-clerking enables the meeting to see the clerking role as a fluid, shared activity, as much as a series of compartments.

At a meeting of Young Friends General Meeting, I observed this as co-clerks Siobhan Haire and Sally Nicholls worked through agenda items in the first session of the day, taking turns to present an item; guide the discernment and write notes; and draft possibilities for a minute. I noted how this way of turn-taking enabled the one seated at the table drafting also to be free to watch (or "read") the meeting, while the other did the standing – at the start, to introduce an item;

and towards the close of discernment to read out the draft minute that they had come up with, receive amendments, confer at the table with her seated colleague, and then stand to read back – this reading out itself being part of the writing process.

This observation reminded me that while Friends in general, as well as those in this survey, might see a separation between "chairing" and "minute-writing" ("reading" and "writing"), it is both possible and likely that the co-clerking approach enables the Friend being tasked with "doing the minutes" also to play a part in "facilitation", or reading the sense of the meeting, and the one "chairing" or "facilitating" to be active in the writing, too.

Afterword

Quaker appointments are traditionally for a three-year term, which provides a key tool to enable both a sustainable and equal organisation. The findings here on co-clerking suggest there is a similar value in sharing the appointment. In terms of holding the worshipful basis for making decisions, such an arrangement provides a basis from which to propagate a wider understanding of the approach to decision-making, with a range of Friends gaining the chance to contribute to the life of their meetings.

There is a view that clerks are specially gifted people. People who have not served as a clerk seem very often to regard those who have as set apart. "Oh, I could never do that", said one Friend. "I'm not academic enough." "I just don't know how he does it", was another comment on a current clerk in their meeting. "I think he's amazing." Could there be a possibility that this unique capacity to clerk might have something to do with the help or presence of God? If so, that suggests the possibility that it is open to anyone to clerk, not just the rare individual.

In Quaker faith and practice, there should be no rush to a minute; and no clerk should be a lonely leader. The expression "the matter is before the meeting" may be the best first lesson for a new clerk to learn. There seems, then, another benefit to the collaborative approach to minute-writing offered by co-clerking. With a whole group quietly supporting the work, the sight of two heads bent over a draft at the clerk's table at the moment of scribing is a reminder that this drafting work is never done alone. Indirectly, the physical presence of two at the table, I suggest, provides a reminder of the invisible other presence, too.

CHAPTER 5:

Reading and writing

Reading and writing

Clerks are scribes, eliciting text from speech, writing from the spoken word. Unlike most scribes, however, their role is to do this not with an individual, but with a group. Quaker usage sees clerks as reading the "sense" of the meeting and initiating and developing the draft of what is to become that group's text: a record of its decisions.

Until now, we have been looking at a religious understanding of the Quaker approach to decision-making. In this chapter, I take a "social practice" understanding of the same thing to see how the way in which Quakers use reading and writing as part of making decisions might show something of the values that underpin the approach.

This chapter is in five sections, considering:

- What is the social practice of literacy?
- What happens with different points of view – changing "domains"?
- How does the collective composition of a Quaker minute work?
- Why do Quakers read aloud, and what is the effect?
- In what way does the Quaker style of writing give expression to Quaker values?

I conclude with an example of stories that do not get written – recalling the value given in Quaker faith to the unspoken, as well as the unwritten.

1. Literacy as a social practice

For a long time, literacy has tended to be seen as something children do or do not learn in school: a set of skills, acquired and developed in a classroom, taught, supported and assessed by trained teachers. National literacy levels have long been used as one index of a country's state of development, and a "great divide" view of literacy versus illiteracy has dominated. An early change to this set of assumptions came in 1957 from Richard Hoggart, who chose for the first volume of his memoirs the title *The uses of literacy*. A couple of decades later, academic studies developed the idea of literacy as something people use in social relationships. This work came to be called the

"New Literacy Studies" and crossed disciplines, bringing together linguists, sociologists, historians, anthropologists – and adult literacy practitioners, such as myself.

The phrase "social literacies" came into favour, because an individual may have recourse to different kinds of literacy for different situations, and literacy use varies with context. People use reading and writing in one culture at one time differently from the same period in another culture, or the same culture at another time. In addition, individuals in a given place, at a given time, may move between different domains in their lives. A "domain" is a social setting with its own micro-culture, so to speak. In a single day, an individual may move between the domains of home, public transport, employment, and sport, for example. Within each there may be expectations of how and when to read and write texts – whether these be membership cards, travel passes, contracts, timetables or notes on the kitchen table, so that literacy is not so much a collection of discrete skills as a social practice. In the words of a leading figure in this set of ideas, Brian Street, this insight was "both banal and profound":

> It is banal, in the sense that once we think about it it is obvious that literacy is always practised in social contexts and that even the school, however "artificial" it may be accused of being in its ways of teaching reading and writing, is also a social construction... The notion is... also profound in that it leads to quite new ways of understanding and defining what counts as literacy (Street 2001, p. 18).

In their account of a nine-year study into people's everyday uses of reading and writing, David Barton and Mary Hamilton summarised the "social theory of literacy" as composed of three elements: practices, events and texts. Literacy practices, they proposed, are mixed up with values, attitudes, feelings and social relationships. We infer these practices from literacy events. These events are activities in which literacy has a role, both written and spoken language are involved, and there is some use of texts. A written text is just one part of an occasion when reading and writing is going on. By looking

Reading and writing

closely at what is happening on such occasions, observers can find something of a group's values and attitudes (Barton and Hamilton 1998, pp. 10–13).

Since literacy practices change along with societies, the way we do things today is not immutable. The document or text produced, whether hand-addressed envelope, email message or a glossy brochure, correctly spelt or full of typos, is the tangible result of a process. Literacy, thought about in this way, is no longer the attribute of individuals, the technical skill, the "correct" way to produce or consume writing: it is a community resource, a way of behaving, with choices being made as to how and when to make use of it and variations of style and voice according to purpose and audience.

This offers us a lens, I think, with which to notice something about uses of literacy in Quaker meetings for worship for business. At these meetings, participants are not only worshipping and making decisions; they are reading and writing, as a group. And their literacy practices, for the times we live in now, are unusual and worth noticing. Behind this, we may also infer the values at work in the specific social domain of a Quaker community.

2. Changing domains

It was not until 2002, a year after first visiting a Quaker meeting for worship for business, that I began attending weekly meetings for worship. Barely a couple of years after that, I applied for membership, became a Quaker, and not long after was appointed to the role of clerk for my local meeting. For the next three years I learned what clerking felt like from the other side of the table. In the early days, the thing that struck me most was how differently I felt about the group's silence as the clerk writes. Instead of feeling calm and awed, I felt that I was keeping people waiting.

In social practice terms, I had brought with me assumptions about literacy practices from other domains in my life. To me, the silence in the room made me feel anxious; I was the minutes secretary, holding things up. In the many secular meetings I had experienced over the years, the aim was to get on with the business. The last thing that participants in those committees, working parties and board meetings (including me) expected to do was wait for the minutes secretary to catch up. A key exception to this was in the editorial meetings of the literacy newspaper *Write first time*, publishing three issues a year between 1975 and 1985 of writings by adult literacy students, who were also among the membership of the editorial groups. In those meetings, adult literacy teachers like me learned the value of practices such as reading the minutes aloud at the start of each meeting.

In the Quaker setting, I had to get used to the expectation that everyone there was not just waiting, but at the same time "upholding" the clerk, and that was their job. "Trust the process", Friends would advise me. Sometimes, I did. Later, I came to have faith that we were all in this together. Later still, I recognised more fully that the event in which I was a participant was a time of worship and that, as my friend Caroline Nursey had told me years earlier, the minute I was writing was not mine, but the meeting's:

> The clerk/scribe is not the author. The author is the whole group, including God. She or He isn't dictating to me, but God is part of the meeting. What I'm trying to do is scribe the sense of the meeting (Caroline Nursey, quoted in Mace 2002, p. 109).

During the period that I was reading the responses to my first questionnaire in 2011 and staying at Woodbrooke Quaker Study Centre, I fell into conversation one evening with Sheila Houldin, at the time a Friend in Residence there. What we talked about was a shared experience. Both of us, it seems, had found the activity of drafting minutes during the meeting surprisingly stressful. From six years' experience as assistant clerk, two as clerk, Sheila captured it in these words:

> The moment it was time for me to draft, I would get a kind of stage fright. It's shared, but you are the focus. It's a kind of performance. I'd get home and would have trouble reading my own writing to make a fair copy from because my hand had trembled so much. And then there were the arrows and

circles I'd added in, for the extra bits that Friends had asked to put in. It was terrible.

This response of Sheila's chimed with my own. In a serious sense, we were both having difficulty with literacy. Before I had become a clerk myself, it had felt comfortable to wait while the clerk or clerks wrote on our behalf. I felt quiet, respectful, grateful. When it became my turn to sit on the other side of the table, however, I found I had nothing to write. Or rather, I had notes, but I could not read them. I experienced moments of panic. I felt sure Friends must be running out of patience.

Once, a very experienced Friend offered to sit by me and be a temporary assistant. Later, another Friend served as assistant clerk, and when his other commitments allowed he certainly helped. Somehow, of course, I did draft the minutes, read them out, and gain acceptance for them. Friends in my meeting certainly expressed a similar mix of respect, gratitude and kindliness that I had myself felt towards other clerks. But I did go home sometimes with a sense of having failed: an echo, strangely, of what I had heard others voicing years earlier in adult literacy classes. Having spent most of my working life writing, and teaching others to do so too, I had regarded myself as reasonably competent at the thing. Letters, minutes, poems, reports, books: I had done them all. What was the problem?

From the point of view of social practice, there is a simple answer. Both Sheila and I were confused by a shift in literacy practice from a secular community or workplace domain to a religious one: a confusion echoed by one or two of the clerks quoted in the last chapter. As we have seen, the Quaker literacy practice of composing minutes, unlike this activity in other settings, assumes there will be some divine connection. Linda Craig gave me an account of experiencing this. As she told me, she was clerking a meeting for worship for business. The agenda item concerned the collection of money for good causes at the end of the meeting for worship; in particular, whether the meeting should give up collecting for the church itself, Britain Yearly Meeting. (It seems that when this was the cause of the week, the collection did not yield much money, whereas in the weeks when it was a charity such as Oxfam or

Amnesty International, it did.) There was, as she put it, "fairly robust ministry on both 'sides'" and then there came a point where she felt she had to try a minute.

> And this is the bit I remember really clearly. I didn't know, as I picked up the pen, what I was going to write. I didn't even have the shape of the minute in my head. And then the words seemed to just flow. The result was probably a compromise, but the minute was accepted immediately by all, with very little change suggested.

"I do believe", she concluded, "that something other than oneself (call it God or the Spirit) is involved at these times."

3. Collective composition

At a business meeting, Quakers expect to write a collectively agreed text. To do this, they ask one or two to take on the role of scribing for the group, with the task of producing a wording that may express the sense of those present. The meeting, for its part, is expected to give assent to this, a text they have heard but not yet read visually. When the clerk reads out a draft minute, those present are expected not just to listen, but also to contribute: either by suggesting amendments or by showing their acceptance of what they hear. Reading binds together with writing; as the draft becomes an acceptable finished text, the group takes ownership of it.

At the Milford Haven business meeting described in Chapter 2, I saw an example of this. Friends had agreed on the fund for which they would use money raised from the entry charges and sales at the exhibition, but had not yet specified what they would spend this fund on. One Friend pointed out that the meeting needed to decide this at some point. Others suggested they were running out of time and should deal with this matter at a later date. The clerk read out an initial draft minute:

> We agree that money from ticket sales, recipe books, crafts and donations should form a bicentenary fund.

Reading and writing

Another Friend suggested that the minute needed to record the second part of their decision, too (i.e. the decision to decide the financial detail later). The meeting clerk then offered additional wording and the meeting accepted the minute as amended:

> We agree that money from ticket sales, recipe books, crafts and donations should form a bicentenary fund, *the use of which will be decided later.*

At a business meeting I witnessed in Edinburgh, there was another moment when the meeting agreed to an amendment to the clerk's draft minute. The item concerned a review of the custom of holding an all-age meeting for worship. The meeting first heard a report from the elders on this, which expressed appreciation for the work of the children's committee and an interest in encouraging more of this kind of worship. Several points were made. The clerk then stood and read out a possible draft minute:

> We confirm our thanks to the Children's Committee for their work, and affirm the minute from elders which we have found helpful.
>
> We agree to support the continuation of all-age meeting for worship with the current arrangements, which have attracted greater numbers to attend than previously when it was held in the hall.

The clerk sat down and another Friend then stood up. He said:

> That seems fine to me, but I would like to add something. Having it up in the main meeting room once a month has made it a more worshipful event – rather than it being a [children's meeting] bookended by a bit of silence – and I would like a recognition of that. If we could find a way of adding that to the minute I think that would be good.

The clerk then offered a draft addition to the last sentence of the minute so that it would read:

> We agree to support the continuation of all-age meeting for worship with the current arrangements, which have attracted greater numbers to attend than previously when it was held in the hall *and is becoming a more worshipful meeting for both adults and children alike.*

The meeting accepted this.

It is worth noting the purpose – and effect – of these two amendments. The first served to ensure that the meeting would remember that it still had work to do regarding the use of the funds raised. The second clarified the reason for agreeing to the continued holding of all-age meeting (not just because of the resulting increased numbers but because of a difference in the quality of worship).

4. Reading aloud

Unlike other Christian or Christian-based churches, Quakers in the liberal tradition do no collective recitation – of prayers, creeds or hymns. However, in today's culture of largely individual and silent reading and writing, Quaker meetings for worship for business include another unusual reading activity: namely, a good deal of reading aloud – or rather, for most participants, listening to texts being read aloud – not just of the draft minute, but of much else too. Apart from the reader, all present are both spectator and audience to this: as one in the group reads out the text and the rest listen – sometimes, if it is a report, following the words on photocopies of it at the same time. This is such an ordinary activity in Quaker business meetings that no-one comments on it. Yet, at least in my own experience, it is not a very usual one in other meetings, where, more commonly, the secretary circulates papers beforehand and people are either expected to have already read these or the person reporting on an item simply "speaks to" their report.

The sound of a voice reading aloud, however imperfectly, holds a certain power. For the listener, each experience has a slightly different quality, according to the place and context. For a child

Reading and writing

listening to an adult reading a story, there is a kind of intimacy. For an audience listening to a poet reading their work, there can be a touch of theatre. For a congregation in church, the reader at the lectern is doing holy work.

Quakers too read out loud from a book as part of the worship meeting; but the book is not a sacred scripture, fixed in time. It is the "book of discipline", *Quaker faith & practice*. In the early stage of a meeting for worship, it is common for an elder to rise out of the silence, read something to the meeting from this book and then sit down, allowing the group to continue listening to the words in the silence that follows. This also happens at the start of business meetings. It engages a group at the same time in reading the same text, and in so doing they recall a common discipline, a committed faith, a shared purpose.

How do elders and others choose which bit to read? From my own area meeting, Sarah Eilbeck described it to me as a choice that can be both accidental and "led":

> Lyn was supposed to choose the reading, but after meeting for worship asked me to, as she had forgotten to give our contribution on the discussion on central works to the clerks and needed to write it out and give it to them.
>
> While the clerks were preparing for area meeting, I picked up a copy of *Quaker faith & practice* and it seemed to fall open at Chapter 10. Looking at the chapter heading – "Belonging to a Quaker Meeting" – it seemed appropriate to choose a reading from it and I felt drawn to 10.05, which is why I read it.
>
> It felt like the same process that I sometimes use to choose a reading from *Quaker faith & practice* for reading at the beginning of meeting for worship as part of my role as elder, being led by the Spirit.

As I have suggested, a lot of other reading aloud goes on in Quaker business meetings. We have already noted how the clerk sometimes reads out the draft minute more than once before a finished version is accepted – and will often then read it out in full one more time, committing everyone in the room to a co-authorship of it.

At the Gloucestershire meeting to which Sarah was reading, I noted these other documents being read aloud:

- a letter from the AM coordinator for children and young people asking the meeting to convey a concern about the level of conviviality proposed for this year's Junior Yearly Meeting (read by the clerk)
- a section of the trustees' report (read out by the clerk to the trustees)
- a report from a conference of Quakers in Criminal Justice attended by the AM chaplain to the local prison (read out by that Friend)
- an extract from a funding application from Young Friends General Meeting (read by the clerk).

In short, the meeting listened to parts or whole texts from a book of church discipline, a management report, a conference record and a financial document. These are not bedtime stories, poetry or scripture. They may contain eloquence, but they are not intended to be works of literature. They have authors, but they are not personal writings.

Why do Quakers do this? Is it a matter of honouring an inherited tradition from a time when only a minority would have been literate? If so, it certainly says something powerful about a commitment to equality and inclusivity. Or is it something a little deeper, to do with a Quaker testimony to "the truth"? The activity of silent reading is a phenomenon that only came into common use at the end of the 19th century – barely a hundred and fifty years ago. David Vincent, a historian of literacy, puts the case more bluntly: "Most printed words found their way into the minds of most of the populations of the past through their ears rather than their eyes" (Vincent 2000, p. 94).

For one person, with literacy skills, to read aloud a newspaper or letters to another, or to a group without those skills, is a much older and more widespread practice in the communities and households of Britain than the practice of individual reading. In addition, for most early Quakers speech would have been primary; the written word a second-best form, necessary to get the word out further. Historian Kate Peters discusses this. She suggests how Friends might have placed more trust in the spoken than the written word. A reader reading privately, after all, might interpret a written tract differently to the author's intentions and authors would thereby lose control over interpretation, whereas "public preaching allowed speakers to respond to questions and audience reaction" (Peters 2005, p. 21). Only a handful of these Quakers were authors of tracts (and even fewer were women), but many were powerful speakers.

In the 1650s, as Kate Peters goes on to explain, the leading Quaker Margaret Fell, for example, wrote tracts to be sent further afield than she could travel, and wrote them in the expectation of them being read aloud. Evidence from the records makes clear (p. 69) that Quaker writings were distributed and sold to be used publicly, read aloud by Quaker ministers, in market places and churchyards, like prepared sermons. So when one of her writings was read out at a meeting in Sunderland in August 1655, one listener, William Caton, could almost hear Margaret Fell herself in the room. A former member of the Fell household, then aged about nineteen, he wrote to her later: "truly my hart was much broken to hear thy voice, it was so pure and pleasant to my eares" (p. 31).

It is true that the effect of listening in a group to a text read aloud is likely to be very different in today's cultural context from how it was in William Caton's time. And yet, just as he felt his spirit stirred that August day in 1655, it may still be possible to feel the spirit stirred by a reading aloud in a way that individual silent reading cannot do. In conversation with a Friend about this, we discovered a common experience when it came to reading back the minutes of a meeting. "At the time," she said, "the minute feels huge. Later, when I read it on email or the noticeboard, it seems very small." For those sitting in the huge gathering of a Yearly Meeting session, the sound of the concluding minute being read out could almost have the status of an oracle. A month later, the same typeset text among others scattered on a kitchen table may seem a very short matter, one among many, almost a piece of bureaucracy. The voice of the reader, the company of listeners, the stillness before and after are no longer there. The context has shifted.

As you would expect, Quakers do have one or two other reading practices besides listening to texts read to a group. For study purposes, for example, a common approach can be to work in a small group to read a text together thoughtfully and discuss responses. *Lectio divina* has been a part of the Christian tradition for centuries, an active approach that takes the reader through stages, allowing them to get in touch with the Spirit that brought the words on the page in the first place. Ginny Wall offers a clear summary of the idea and the process (Wall 2012, pp. 29–30); she describes how the reader reads "not so much with the mind as with the heart". Three months after Yearly Meeting Gathering 2011, for example, I was in a circle of six Friends applying this approach. We spent half an hour reading aloud, then silently, the final minute. We identified words that spoke to us, meditated on them, allowed for breath and pause between sentences. In giving time to hear, absorb, taste and wonder about what we had read, there was the sense of something in which we were all of us participants: a gathered stillness.

Two reflections on reading

These observations on Quaker reading practices have led me to consider two issues that may be worth exploring further:

Appropriate timing and frequency for listening to texts read aloud

It seems a balance is needed. At the meeting quoted earlier, Colin Gerard, the clerk to the trustees, read out some but not all of the ten-page trustees' report. As he wrote to me later:

> Reading out the whole of the trustee report would have been too much. Friends might have had trouble staying awake. If Friends want to know who's had a new boiler put in their meeting house they can read it for themselves. But I do think some of these things should be read out. You can say it's all in the packs, but no-one's going to read it.

In theory, reading aloud enables all to hear a text at the same time.

Are there times when not everyone can hear? Is it an approach for which Friends could consciously develop skills?

The uses made of reading minutes
A lot of time and care goes into composing minutes collectively. What kind of practices go into the reading back of the resulting texts? Who reads them? When and how?

5. Plain writing

For anyone interested in accessible language, there are I think two lovely things about the style of Quaker minute-writing. There is no written rule to say that this is how it should be done, but at clerk training courses at Woodbrooke participants learn that this is the expected way of writing; and from clerks who have longer experience in Quaker ways, newcomers learn it as a style that is encouraged.

First is the use of the active voice. These two examples allow us to compare the result of this usage with the passive conventions of minute-writing.

Active voice	Passive voice
1. We have considered the matter of the choice of paint for the gates.	1. The matter of the choice of paint for the gates has been considered.
2. Mary attended the meeting.	2. The meeting was attended by Mary.

In the first example, the active voice tells you who did the considering of the paint question ("we", i.e. those present at the meeting), but the passive voice leaves you to guess who considered it. In the second, we know immediately from the active version that it was Mary who attended the meeting; in the passive version of the same statement, while it is true that we do find that out, we have to wait until the end of the sentence. The use of the active voice in writing minutes means making a priority of saying who it is who has taken responsibility for taking the action – of considering or attending. And it is a lot easier to read.

In everyday speech, we hardly ever use the passive, though legal professionals tend to, especially in courtrooms. However, it is a common feature of formal and scientific writing and is widely used in minute-writing. In fact, in some quarters today it is still promoted as the only proper way to write minutes. According to one source providing training materials on this (Citizens Advice Bureau 2010), there are "three main elements" of good minute-writing in the public and voluntary sectors. These are:

- write impersonally (i.e. without saying who said what)
- write in the passive – neutral and unbiased; and
- use the past tense – because it will be read as a record in the future.

Although this approach is beginning to feel a little outdated in most organisations, the general tendency seems to be the same as it was a generation ago. For example, Jan Burnell, author of one published guidebook, tells her readers in no uncertain terms that

> use of the passive helps to emphasise the corporate nature of the minutes. To say "It was decided" is less personal than to say "We decided" (Burnell 2004, p. 48).

In another guide on minute-writing, Joanna Gutmann clearly sees it differently, arguing that "the active voice is shorter, more direct and more easily understood than the passive voice". She still prefers an impersonal usage for her example of this: "The committee decided" rather than "it was decided by the committee" (Gutmann 2001, p. 128).

The use of the present tense seems also to be a distinctive feature of Quaker minutes, though usually kept for the part of the minute that shows a decision and an action to follow it. The simplest example may occur at the start of a local business meeting, when there is a decision to take about which Friends will attend the area meeting. A typical minute to emerge might read:

> *We appoint* Jane Grey, George Wolf and Anisha Gupta to

Reading and writing

represent this meeting at the area meeting for worship for business on Saturday 21 May at Anytown Quaker Meeting House *and ask* Anisha Gupta to give a brief oral report of the meeting after meeting for worship on Sunday 22 May.

A more extended form would be a minute for discernment, in which the areas about which we had feelings, inspirations, or ideas might occupy more space. Whether it be a minute from a meeting of hundreds of Friends or one of just a handful, the same pattern occurs. By and large, the three parts of such a minute consist of:

We have considered so-and-so;
We feel (this) and are concerned about (that); and
We ask (ourselves, or such an individual or group) to do x, y or z about it.

The first of these three may seem to be a past tense, but is actually written in the present perfect, in which a past action is seen to be active in the present. It is a standard preferred use in Quaker minutes (though some feel it is not as widely used as it could be).

Why this insistence on a present tense? You might feel that the three-part whole could just as well be put into the past tense: as in "We agreed", "We felt" and "We asked". But think back, for a moment, to how the minutes of Yearly Meeting and Meeting for Sufferings discussed in earlier chapters might be later read – and heard – elsewhere. When those who travelled to those gatherings get back home to their local meetings and are asked to read out the minute to those present, what difference does that present tense make there? Like others, these minutes are not only a matter of historical record: they are a living call to action, inviting ownership, suggesting that effectively God, within the listeners, is asking this of them now.

Names and signatures

There is a sense of the personal in the use of the active voice. But when it comes to recording those present at the meeting, Quakers prefer to leave out names. It is usual to record just the number of people present (as in: 12 present). American Quaker Sharon Hoover offers two reasons for this:

> The Spirit may work on any one of us as individuals or on us as a body during or after a discussion, so that later in the discussion, or the next time we gather, we are in a different place. Also, although we listen to the wisdom of other Friends, we are finally looking for the leading of the Spirit, not for the position of a particular person (Hoover 2011, p. 19).

At the same time, there is a general view that it is a good idea to sign minutes – for the archive, for legal reasons. Friends asked about this are a little vague. Guidance on this to clerks simply says what they should do, not why:

> It is good practice for the rough minutes to be signed at the meeting's conclusion. This also gives the clerk authority to sign any fair copy once it is certain it has been correctly transcribed ($Qf&p$ 3.15).

It would be interesting to know, in practice, just how many clerks do sign minutes, and if so, with what understanding of the reason. From a brief discussion with Friends attending a Woodbrooke weekend course for clerks, I found there to be a fair number of questions to explore. Asked "Do Friends here sign minutes?", just two or three out of the circle of some twenty present immediately said yes, of course.

One said no, she had never signed any minutes, "but we do have to with archive minutes". Another agreed that "there is a legal correctness to signing". For another, the feeling of signing the typed copy seems to "fix it" for her. But this raised an uncertainty. Did that mean she signed the copy she had printed out at home? One person said he felt "uncomfortable" at this idea. "You don't know what the clerk is signing", he said. This raised the comment from another speaker that "The spirit of the meeting can be made more inclusive by the way the clerk handles these things". Two people mentioned that what they did (as the clerk did at the local business

Reading and writing

meeting reported in Chapter 2) was sign the last meeting's minutes at the start of the next one. As one put it, "Signing minutes keeps me honest". And perhaps that's where the clue lies. For the meeting to witness the clerk signing the text they have made reassures all present that their text is complete and will not be altered. The clerk signs for the meeting. It is a symbol of commitment.

Changing technologies

For the first three hundred years of the Religious Society of Friends, minutes were usually handwritten. Over the last fifty, it has become more likely for the clerk to take home a rough, handwritten completed draft and copy-type the fair version – these days on a word processor. More recently, slowly but surely, the laptop is making its appearance in the meeting itself.

There are Friends who express discomfort about this change. (The laptop screen might hide the face? The tap of the keyboard might distract?) Such discomfort is apparently not new. More than half a century ago, the move from handwriting to typing evidently made Friends very concerned: Ted Milligan recalled an example for me from his time as clerk for Reading Meeting in the 1950s. The meeting had come to the end of the minute book. Ted suggested that instead of buying a replacement, they should buy a lever arch file, and he as clerk could type out the minutes and put them in there. "It caused an uproar!", he said:

> People talked of the beauty of handwriting, the loss it would mean. I remember saying something like, "If Friends are concerned about setting a precedent, it might help to know that the minutes for Meetings for Sufferings have been typed since 1928." At which Howard R. Smith stood up and said, "It may be all very well for the Meeting for Sufferings, *Teddy*, but that is *not* alright for our preparative meeting.

In the end, however, as Ted told me, the meeting did move to typing.

A growing number of clerks today seem to agree with Geoffrey Johnson's feeling that he "could not do without" his laptop. From the first survey for this book several, like Mark Bitel, reported preparing pre-drafts beforehand and then redrafts and amendments on the keyboard during the meeting. (As Mark saw it, this makes for shorter meetings as "I can type on my laptop faster than I can write!".)

One minute

From her snapshot of her own local meeting for worship for business, Deborah Rowlands suggested how the true spirit of a meeting's work may lie hidden within the written minute. Together with the story behind it, this offers us an example of a literacy event in which context and relationships, listening and speaking play a big part, and what is going on is a great deal more than just somebody doing a bit of reading or writing. The context in the business meeting so far had been an agenda of three or four reports to listen to and accept, a financial policy to understand and think about: an occasion when there was a good deal of thinking, discerning and care. And then this item, with a double problem to solve, and (once a solution was found) a good deal of laughter. As Deborah told me:

> Our meeting is held in premises in the middle of town. Most of the week, it is used as a centre for people with learning difficulties. We just have the use of it on a Sunday. Many travel for miles to get there. The question we were facing was that recently, the keyholder had forgotten to bring the key one Sunday. What could we do if that happened again?
>
> It was an item that combined the two issues of security and money. People were worried about the safety of the collection left in a box, in a cupboard, so we had agreed that there would be a rota for one Friend to take it home each week. And then the idea came. The Friend who suggested it is usually very quiet in business meetings. Her question was: couldn't we just join the box with the key? Whoever took the box with the collection home could also take the key home. And they wouldn't forget to bring back the key, because they have to bring the collection box back.

The two problems could be solved in one: making sure the key would be passed on and looking after the collection between meetings. The meeting apparently broke into laughter. Such a simple idea! The Friend who had proposed it, who usually said little in business meetings, had made the crucial contribution. For another, usually quiet Friend, new to Quaker ways, the delight in the group at this solution offered light relief after the more serious way things had been going until then. "Sometimes," as Deborah put it to me, "a quip or joke can offer just the feeling needed in the midst of the more ponderous bits of a meeting, when it can seem that the only people to speak are those who can talk in long sentences." The meeting accepted a minute that simply recorded the problem, the comment and the resolution:

> We note that monies are sometimes left in the Canolfan (in our box). We think this is not good practice. We agree that the keyholder will hold the key in the money box, too, together with the emergency information.

The story helps suggest the delicate balance to be struck between words and spirit. From the point of view of literacy as a social practice, the written minutes from a Quaker business meeting are just a part of a literacy event in which participants are trying to reach unity. In that sense, the written result might best be seen as the souvenir of a religious experience, as much as the formal record of a decision.

Two reflections on writing

The composition process of Quaker minute-writing is fascinating. There are at least two areas that I think would be interesting to research further:

The nature of amendments
In both the meetings mentioned in this chapter, the amendments offered were additions to the draft. As far as I recall from my visits to local and area business meetings, both in the course of this study

and in my own area, amendments nearly always follow this pattern: they consist of words that need adding rather than deleting. Is the pattern as widespread as this seems to suggest (and if so, are the reasons for it to do with Quaker values)?

The change of the composition process over time
What changes may have happened in the balance between silence and speech, speech and writing over time? Is it true (as I think it may be) that the text of a meeting's minutes today is longer than that of the same meeting, say, a hundred years ago? If so, has any of this been to do with a change in writing technology (taking longer to write in longhand than on the keyboard of a laptop, for instance) or has there been a change in values behind it?

Afterword

During the research for this book, I had a discussion with other literacy specialists at an annual conference of Research and Practice in Adult Literacy (later published in their journal (Mace 2012)). This discussion helped me see something more clearly. The literacy practices of Quaker business meetings contain an effort to live Quaker values. These practices hold a commitment to at least two of four key Quaker testimonies: equality, simplicity, peace and truth.

Taken together, Quaker literacy practices reveal a commitment to the values of equality and simplicity – key principles in Quaker faith and practice. The group responsibility for composing a record of decision (the minute); the direct and simple style of writing favoured for this record; the care for slow reading and for reading by ear, as it were, in theory at least ensures that anyone and everyone can participate in the texts that need to be written and read – however limited their literacy skills, however small the confidence of the individual in their abilities to be "clever" at reading and writing.

Meanwhile, so much goes on in a Quaker business meeting that is never written – and has a spiritual value of another kind. Deborah Rowlands' meeting felt no need to record the discernment that led to their decision. An apparently "mundane" matter had provided the means for the group to find a solution, and no more needed to be said.

Reading and writing

Since the 17th century, Quakers have always placed importance on well-written records kept safely in archival conditions: records not only of decisions but also, when it has felt important, of discernment and, of course, guidance; whether it be a safeguarding policy or a job description for a newsletter editor, a leaflet or an invitation. However, within the literacy practices of the approach to decision-making there is also faith in non-verbal forms of expression, in silence itself, and in the unwritten. Reading and writing are only a small part of the story. Words can only do so much. These stanzas from a poem by Carol Ann Duffy (Duffy 2002) seem to me to capture something of this commitment to the spirit inherent in the literacy practices of Quaker business meetings:

> No rules written to guide you,
> I write them white,
> words on the wind,
> traced with a stick where we walk on the sand.
>
> No news written to tell you,
> I write it white,
> foam on a wave
> as we lift up our skirts in the sea, wade,
>
> see last gold sun behind clouds,
> inked water in moonlight.
> No poems written to praise you,
> I write them white.

Whether spoken or written, the poet tells us, language is always transient; the news I really wish to tell you is beyond words; beauty is found in the inexpressible; poetry (like religious worship) can sometimes put the unexpected together and find – or make – new meanings.

In this chapter, I have considered some of the distinctive ways in which Quakers in Britain use literacy today to take a meeting through the process of decision-making. It is an impression only, but it does seem to me that a great deal more text use goes on today than in the past. Minute files today contain many more pages than minute books from a century ago. The community's literacy practices compete with the stillness necessary for worshipful discernment and, arguably, there is sometimes a case for less text altogether.

CHAPTER 6:

Learning

Learning

Quakers aspire to make decisions worshipfully. Among the challenges they face in doing this, we have considered several – not least the problem of covering the business in the time allowed. However, two others, less often mentioned, are no less pressing: the sheer practicality of enabling participants to actually meet (with obstacles thrown up by weather and transport); and the need to make more widely known the concepts and principles behind aspiring to worshipful decision-making.

This last chapter begins with creative solutions to the first challenge, explored by two meetings. I then consider how someone with the curiosity I had some ten years ago can find out about the Quaker approach to decision-making, looking at four current approaches to learning. In conclusion, I offer some brief notes and reflections on my own learning from undertaking this study.

Meeting without meeting

The theory of Quaker decision-making is that a decision is arrived at not through debate, argument or persuasion, but through careful listening for a unity. In the course of this, time sometimes needs to be allowed for "threshing out" strong feelings or opinions. These two case studies suggest how it's possible to undertake both threshing and discernment without physically meeting.

Threshing by email
Threshing, as we considered earlier on, is a valuable part of the process of discernment. Sandra Figgess described how her meeting set about a process for doing this without physically meeting. They were wishing to produce a statement on the proposed cuts in public expenditure. Many Friends had a concern about the effects of these cuts. It was clear that some of them were fully occupied with managing their everyday working and family lives and had little spare time for one more meeting. So the meeting agreed to undertake some threshing by email, the purpose of which was to provide a means for all those Friends concerned to thresh out their ideas, opinions and feelings on the matter. They appointed an email clerk, whose role was to ask Friends to focus on the topic and to

send her (and each other) their views, from which she undertook to produce a preliminary draft statement to bring back to the next business meeting for consideration.

Sandra stressed that this exercise was absolutely not a discernment process; rather, it was a form of pre-discernment. The email clerk's task was to gather views and elicit something that the participants might agree seemed to sum these up, and then bring this summary (about two pages long) to the meeting clerks. The process for this topic was started at the December business meeting. The email clerk reported back to the February one. The meeting was then able to use it, together with the consideration of the Friends present, to come to unity on a fully discerned minute.

In the course of this study, the growing use of email in Quaker life has been mentioned to me both as curse and as blessing. There is a fear that too much of our business might be going on behind closed doors, as it were, from one laptop to another, and that these conversations exclude not only those not included in the circulation, but also those who have no computer at home. What Sandra pointed out to me in our phone conversation about this was that a requirement to discern only at a physical meeting of Friends can also be excluding. One of the Friends with expertise in economics and public finance was also the parent of a disabled child, so that while he could easily contribute to an email discussion, he could rarely spare the time for any additional meetings in his week. Oxford Local Meeting produced a protocol for the use of email in this way to prepare an item of concern for business meetings. They saw it, Sandra told me, as a means to do preparatory work on a newly arising complex concern, to take it beyond the "what shall we do about x?" phase into considering more specific proposals. The email clerk was the point of contact for those wishing to participate. The discussion ended with the matter going to clerks for the business meeting's next agenda.

Discernment by telephone conference

But what if transport limits or weather conditions make it impossible for enough Friends to get to a business meeting? Cancelling may only add to the sense of isolation between Friends who are already geographically scattered. It can deprive them not only of necessary decisions, but of the gathered group, the worshipping community. In West Scotland Area Meeting, the prospects for their winter meeting did not look good, so they came up with an alternative. This is how Elizabeth Allen recalled the story in the *Scottish Friend* (February 2011, pp. 17–18):

> In Wigtown on a sunny day in June, we set the dates for Area Meeting for the following year, being mindful that in the winter months it would be prudent to hold our meetings in the city. As the time drew near for bleak December's Area Meeting, sunny June was just a memory and severe weather warnings, road closures, dangerous driving conditions, snow and more snow was the reality. Events were being cancelled everywhere but there was still over one week to go before Area Meeting and there might be a thaw or at least an easing of conditions! Snow continued to fall and emails from Friends in our scattered Local Meetings and from Glasgow suburbs started to arrive in flurries in my mail box. It became evident, even to an eternal optimist like me, that the only people who were going to be at Area Meeting in Glasgow were those who could walk, and even they were going to have difficulty. It looked like we would have to cancel it, or was there something else we could do? Phones were ringing. Friends were talking, bright ideas were in the air and a Meeting for Business by telephone conference emerged as something we might try.
>
> It was simple to set up. The system we chose was one where Friends joined the conference at a pre-arranged time by dialling in and entering a code number. We set a clear time frame for the meeting, one hour, which cost each participant £3. The agenda was redrafted and focused on routine and essential business. Full draft minutes were circulated in advance.
>
> Eleven Friends from seven of our nine Local Meetings took part. During our opening worship 2.84 of *Quaker faith &*

practice was read out and Friends were reminded that God is with us in every place. This was an inspirational moment. We settled into the telephone conference, we dealt with the business and we held together in that worshipful spirit until the end of our meeting.

Reflecting on this, Elizabeth makes three points:

- Friends were "pleasantly surprised" at how well it worked, noting too the "ease of joining in from their own home" compared to their usual long journeys;
- on the other hand, not meeting together meant missing "our time of fellowship";
- by definition, the event excluded those who (for reasons not given) did not participate.

On balance, the area meeting felt they would repeat the arrangement in similar circumstances, and might use it, too, to "clear routine business in advance", giving more time for a topic of special interest. They knew they could not create the same feeling of fellowship that is only possible when a group is in the same place, but they also recognised the benefits in terms of sustainability and inclusiveness in cutting back environmentally costly journeys, which some Friends might not be able to undertake anyway.

Learning

In days of hot contest and bitter controversy the early Friends, knit together by the glorious experience of the Holy Spirit's guidance in all their affairs, *came into the simple understanding* of how their corporate decisions should be made. (*Qf&p* 3.04; my italics)

Many Friends, either because they have never attended a business meeting or have not had the chance to talk over what they have seen, have no idea how decision-making takes place in their meeting. To "come into the simple understanding", as early Friends were apparently able to do, feels an enviable experience, but not an easy one to achieve. Reading the published sources for this book has certainly helped me. After my appointment as a new assistant clerk, attending a Woodbrooke training course for clerks was absolutely invaluable.

But how does anyone in the whole body of Friends, who may have no wish to offer service as a clerk and little time for extra reading, "come into the simple understanding" of how our decisions should be made? There may be many answers. From the study for this book, I suggest here just four: the Friend can learn through osmosis, through social learning, through study or through demonstration.

Osmosis

Simply attending, watching and listening is certainly one way of learning, as Ted Milligan recalled for me. A "birthright, but not a dynastic Quaker", he began attending the monthly meeting with his family at an unusually early age (about age seven, he thought) in Rochester, Kent. "I liked to go", he recalled,

> because it meant travelling over the North Downs on an open-top double-decker bus. During the afternoons, I sat with my parents and drew, though after tea, I tended to drowse.

But it seems that he also took something in of what was going on – something, in particular, about a process of decision-making:

> I firmly believe that I learned most about conduct and clerkship by osmosis. One episode during those years stuck – though it was only long after that I came to realise how important it had been. Margaret Sefton-Jones (a wealthy Friend, who expected others to accept her opinions, as I later discovered) had laid before the meeting a proposal that Paris Meeting should become part of our monthly meeting … Three months later, I went to monthly meeting to see what would happen.
>
> As I remember it, she spoke with great force, and on

resuming her seat, the meeting sank into silence. It remained so. Finally, if I recall it right, one Friend arose and said that it was a proposal which should remain on Friends' minds. And the meeting advanced to its next business.

I recognise the fallibility of my memory, but clearly the absence of argument, the trust of silence, must have made a deep impression, as well as the sensitivity of the Friend (I think it was Wilfrid Dale) who knew the moment to express the meeting's unspoken but united judgement, and thus enable the clerk to present a minute.

It does not matter to me whether or not this is an "objectively accurate" account of what took place at that business meeting that day. What seems so interesting is the way that Ted Milligan felt it had – and the value he placed on its character: the sequence of strong words and the "sinking into silence"; the clerk's sense of the meeting; and last, but not least, his willingness to observe and "sink into" the experience himself.

This openness to learning offers a way for a deep impression to be allowed in to teach. There is humility here, in which the critical mind, so lively and ready to see mistakes and conflict, can be asked to rest, while the spirit attends to the good that is also going on.

Informal learning

These days, many of us come into Quaker faith and practice as adults rather than growing up in it, and it is by learning how the community regulates itself, sends and receives messages, voices and accepts ideas, that we may become part of what the educational theorist Étienne Wenger has called its "community of practice". Learning the ways of behaving and relating in a particular context allows us to acquire a sense of identity in that context. We feel we belong. Given that any individual may be a member of more than one community of practice, this can sometimes feel complicated; it can "require some work to reconcile our different forms of membership" (Wenger 1998, pp. 158–59).

So how do Quakers try to make it simpler for newcomers to learn these things? There is a great deal of attention paid to the importance of cultivating a community life. Looking at the "social practice" of a Quaker meeting (as in Chapter 5) is a reminder that

- *every individual is likely to be a member of various communities*, and that the identity any one of us takes around with us, as some put it, brings these together in a mix;
- *any community will have its own, often unconscious, ways of doing things with reading and writing*, and it helps understanding to make explicit what these ways are – and how they relate to values.

For the curious enquirer, then, it seems it is helpful for Quakers to articulate clearly the practices that are distinctive to their community. In particular, it helps to know the connections they aim to find between divine guidance and decision-making; and it helps to know the relationship they expect to form between the disciplines of business meetings and their founding values of equality and simplicity. Newcomers who want to know more can – and do – learn quite a lot about these connections and this relationship through informal as well as formal learning as they travel together to and from meetings, or meet informally at each other's homes.

Study

There is a lot to be said for study groups: few people, a limited number of meetings, a common purpose. I recall in my own meeting a series of four sessions a group of us held to explore the Quaker testimony to simplicity: our only resource, a collection of short readings on the subject put together by Quaker Home Service. We met for an hour and a half on a Friday lunchtime, and it felt very productive. A similar experience, this time for an hour once a fortnight, brought a second group together to take up the themes of "celebrating our Quaker life", using a booklet of the same title. Each session included a short period of silence, a brief reading aloud of a page or two from the publication, twenty minutes of worship sharing, twenty minutes of free discussion, and five or ten minutes of closing silence.

Studying can take many forms. There are learning opportunities throughout the year from the resources of online learning, day workshops and residential courses provided by the Woodbrooke Quaker Study Centre in Birmingham and Quaker Life in London.

Demonstration

Role-play can provide entertainment as well as teaching points. For some ten years (2001 to 2011) Young Friends General Meeting regularly used this at their meetings – and later, by invitation, to other meetings, which has inspired and supported the continuing effort for corporate discipline in business meetings. YFGM is an organisation for young Quakers aged 18 to 30. They run three weekend gatherings a year, to which newcomers are welcome. The infrequency and the certainty of visitors has meant that for some years now YFGM routinely expects to provide a slot in the weekend programme explicitly allocated to explaining the "business method". Young Friends may already know the Quaker ways, but are glad to be reminded, given the passage of time since the last YFGM event; for those attending a Quaker event for the first time, the session provides an introduction. The session, usually held on Saturday morning before the first formal session, is in the charge of their elders (known as Quintessentials, or Quintys). There will already have been a sociable time on the Friday evening when people get a chance to talk to each other.

At a gathering of some fifty young Friends at YFGM in Oxford Meeting House on a Saturday morning in February 2011, this is what I saw and heard in the twenty minutes or so that followed the initial fifteen minutes of silent worship.

Co-clerks at the table introduced the session – to explain the business method:

> First we are going to experience a meeting as we would not wish it to run, then Rachel will invite you to notice what was wrong about it, from which we will pick out what the features are we try for in our Quaker way of doing business.

Five or six people from the body of the meeting then began to act out "bad behaviour". The first stood to present his item for the agenda

– a rambling account of the need to reduce flood risk in the town. The "clerk" (who had been sitting head bent over her mobile phone, evidently sending a text message) looked up and said, "Um, the matter is before the meeting, Friends."

Four individuals then spoke, without standing or introducing themselves, repeating things already said, interrupting each other, starting off on another subject. The clerk, breaking off from her texting and whispering chat with her co-clerk, looked up and asked: "Is there any more ministry?" After two more rather random opinions and anecdotes, she then said: "Shall we maybe vote on it? If you think we should divert the river, raise your hand." Eighteen or so hands went up and the scene ended (with some laughter from the audience).

Rachel, the elder, then took the floor, inviting comments from all present about what was not right about what was "wrong" with this scene as a meeting for worship for business. From the comments made, she then summarised the positive principles that should be there instead and the rules this meeting would be following in the formal sessions that day:

- items should be prepared before they come to the agenda
- no nitpicking of proposals
- once spoken, trust that you have been heard
- keep to the topic
- we decide without voting: what we are doing is discerning the will of God
- stand up, wait to be asked to speak, say your name
- give space between ministry.

She finished by saying that if someone goes on too long, an elder (or Quinty) is there to say "I think we've heard you, Friend"; and if anyone really feels that things are not going well, they can say "I don't feel that this is a meeting in right ordering".

As I have suggested, attending Yearly Meeting in full session provides a unique, large-scale demonstration of Quaker decision-making. Many Friends report that such experience gives an inspiration to take back to smaller meetings, where, as one Friend put it to me, the value of the disciplines lies in keeping a similar kind of rhythm between speech and stillness.

Concluding notes and reflections

On silence in other places
First and foremost, the Quaker meeting for worship for business is a meeting for worship, as part of which those present find some answers to issues that the group has to deal with. Such a spirit of worship can be sustained if the group is listening for the goodness in what someone is saying, as well as when there is silence. Harvey Gillman restates it this way:

> The aim of the business meeting is to discover the will of God. It is not a matter of bowing to the will of majorities or minorities, and Quakers do not vote: *rather it is an exercise of listening to God through what each person says* (Gillman 2003, p. 70; my emphasis).

In other settings, Quakers sometimes find ways to ask for a few moments' silence at the start of a committee meeting ("just to gather our thoughts") or for a ground rule that says no-one speaks until the meeting chair asks them to, or for an experiment in which they might try offering the minutes secretary a moment or two after each item to check what they intend to put in the minutes. The suggestion that there should be a pause between spoken contributions is one step further. It would be interesting to know how and when, outside Quaker settings, such a suggestion is taken up.

"I hope so"
If Quakers do not vote, how do participants in a meeting for worship for business express their acceptance of the minute? The answer is in the words "I hope so". On first hearing these words murmured in a meeting, a newcomer may be a little bewildered, but after attending a few more of these meetings may simply come to do the same. But how does this Friend discover what the words actually mean? Why, anyway, do those present not simply answer the clerk's question with

the single word "yes"?

One answer is this, from Jane Courtis, a seasoned Friend in my own meeting. Why do we say "I hope so"?, I asked. At the time, we were sitting in a circle at a weekend away for our meeting, at which we had been talking about our decision-making or business method. "Well," said Jane, "I think it is a means to pay respect to the presence in the empty chair." Uncertain, I asked her to say more – and quickly realised there was nothing more to say.

Another Friend, in conversation one evening at Woodbrooke, told me that as far as he was concerned, in writing the minute you're writing ministry, so that to him "I hope so" means "I hope that we have correctly discerned the will of the Holy Spirit".

Helen Rowlands expressed it in these terms:

> It's an expression with an element of provisionality about it. We are not doing all this entirely in our own strength. It's saying: "I think I am understanding this to be God's will, but I know that I can never fully know God, therefore I am trusting that our discernment has taken us to this place, but I'm recognising that we might not have done. I'm registering that we can't know God." And also, it's saying: "This is true for me. And I hope it's true for other Friends, too."

While this seems to be, as Helen says, a "provisional" position, it also suggests (as I see it) a declaration of faith in the ineffable nature of the divine. So "I hope so" holds together both uncertainty and certainty, as well as (in Helen's additional meaning) a wish to connect the individual with all the others in the room. This understanding might make us wish for the expression being heard more loudly next time Friends respond to the question "Is that acceptable?". As Young Friends General Meeting agreed, it also suggests that there needs to be, in Maud Grainger's words,

> enough time for Friends to test that. If we're *hoping*, then we have to have made sure that our process enables us to have the confidence to say that we are.

On writing

Appendix 1 is minute 23 from Yearly Meeting Gathering 2011 in Canterbury. When Lis Burch stood and read out this text and offered it as a draft completed expression of our discernment, many may have noticed that it contained both more and less than the sum of the spoken ministries. Somewhere, between the audible words, the clerks had heard something more. And they had captured it sufficiently well for the gathering to give it acceptance.

For Quakers, writing itself is a process of discernment. Written minutes provide records of a meeting's history of decision-making. At the same time, the concern with producing well-worded writing can, it seems, sometimes soak up the time needed for worshipful discernment. In a literate culture with keyboard skills, there may be a risk of producing too much text. The resulting minutes may seem more like the product of a local government department than that of a religious society.

Carol Ann Duffy's poem *White writing* gives a gentle reminder of this risk: the possibility that in ensuring everything is recorded, every subsection included, the letter may kill and the spirit no longer give life. "Black" writing is valuable. But in the white writing – the kind expressed in ways other than words – can be found other meanings: on the sand, in the shallows, on a wave; writing that the authors may simply "hope" is acceptable to a higher spirit, to the best in ourselves.

This book began with the word "God" and some of the meanings that liberal, unprogrammed Quakers give to this in thinking about the work of managing the Society's affairs, locally or nationally. Understood not only as a religious practice, decision-making calls on participants in a Quaker community to submit to "the long focus", to move beyond individual need or hesitation and find what is good for the gathered group.

Appendix I

Yearly Meeting Gathering 2011 in Canterbury

Minute 23: Economic Justice

How can we renew our commitment to our testimonies of truth, justice, integrity and equality, and discern action to take our witness forward?

We have heard today of a number of initiatives in which our Yearly Meeting and its members are involved: the Ethical Trading Initiative and the work of Quaker Social Action. We have shared something of our experience, ideas and discernment from around the Yearly Meeting.

There are many small steps we can all take, as individuals and as meetings. But we also feel called to work on a larger scale. The global economic system is posited on continued expansion and growth, and in its pursuit of growth it is often unjust, violent and destructive. Several Friends have said "we must move out of our comfort zone", and we have heard that rage and passion may also have a place in our responses.

We need to continue to learn more about how we are influenced and constrained by the economic system. We need to ask the question whether this system is so broken that we must urgently work with others of faith and good will to put in its place a different system in which our testimonies can flourish.

As individuals, and in our meetings, we must return to the place from which testimony comes, to open ourselves to the Spirit and to wait humbly in the light. Together, we can help one another to overcome our inertia.

We rededicate ourselves to a corporate discipline of waiting and opening to the leadings of the Spirit on the issues before us at this yearly meeting. We ask Meeting for Sufferings to keep this in view over the coming year.

Appendix 2

Minute by Meeting for Sufferings, at its meeting held in Friends House, London, Saturday 2 April 2011

S/11/04/ 4: *Boycott, divestment and sanctions (Israel/Palestine)*
Further to minute S/11/02/ 4 of 5 February 2011, we receive minutes on this matter from the following Area Meetings: Southern Marches (paper S/11/04/mc i a), Sussex East (i b), Surrey & Hampshire Border (i c), Swarthmoor (i f), North London (i g), Cambridgeshire (i h), East Cheshire (i i), Ipswich & Diss (i j), North West London (i k), Bristol (i l), Hampshire & Islands (i m), Devon (i n) and Manchester & Warrington (i o) and North Cumbria (i p).

Our assistant clerk has summarised the Area Meeting minutes received, and we have returned to our consideration of the issues raised in the papers received at our last meeting (paper S/11/02/A prepared by Marigold Bentley, Assistant General Secretary of Quaker Peace & Social Witness (QPSW), the Kairos Palestine Document *A moment of truth* (paper S/11/02/B), and the Quaker Council for European Affairs Discussion Paper entitled *Responses to the call for boycott, divestment and sanctions* (S/11/02/C).

We have heard of the responses of Jewish Peace Groups within Israel. We hear these Israeli citizens risk being criminalised by their own government if they actively support the Palestinian call for cultural and economic boycott. We were informed that most Jewish Israeli Peace Groups support the boycott of settlement goods, and only some support a boycott of Israel.

A just peace for Palestine means security for Israel too, and nonviolent protests by both Israelis and Palestinians for the end of the occupation are heartening to observe.

For nine years Quakers have been witnessing individually and through the Ecumenical Accompaniment Programme in Palestine and Israel (EAPPI) to the human rights abuses of the military occupation of the Palestinian Territories. Today we have considered whether we should add nonviolent action to our witnessing – not as punishment or revenge, but as an external pressure to achieve change.

Appendix 2

We understand the history and the trauma of the past, but it is the Israelis who are the stronger and they need to make the changes.

John Woolman's words (*Quaker faith & practice* 26.61) remind us of the powerful sense we have of being brothers and sisters with people of other faiths. There are three main faiths in this part of the world, and we want to proceed in ways which allow dialogue to continue. We consider we should now act publicly and, well-informed, be able to explain our action to others – because people matter more than territory, and because we approach others with a desire for peace.

Difficult decisions taken by us today can be reversed. The request for boycott comes from those who will suffer most, but a decision for boycott will give hope to Palestinians and support to those in Israel who are working for peace.

In face of the armed oppression of poor people and the increasing encroachment of the illegal settlements in the West Bank, we cannot do nothing.

Our hearts are full of compassion for Israelis and Palestinians, all of whom are suffering from the effects of the occupation.

We are clear then that it would be wrong to support the illegal settlements by purchasing their goods. We therefore ask Friends throughout Britain Yearly Meeting to boycott settlement goods, until such time as the occupation is ended.

We are not at this time proposing to boycott goods from Israel itself, being unwilling to jeopardise continuing dialogue with Israelis and British Jews.

We pray fervently for both Israelis and Palestinians, keeping them together in our hearts. We hope they will find an end to their fears and the beginning of their mutual co-existence based on a just peace. And so we look forward to the end of the occupation and the end of the international boycott. We envisage our future relationship with both peoples as one of loving and generous co-operation.

Although we unite in this decision, we recognise that Friends have different views, and we must treat one another tenderly.

BIBLIOGRAPHY

Allen, Beth, *Ground and spring: foundations of Quaker discipleship* (Swarthmore Lecture). London: Quaker Books, 2007.

Allen, Elizabeth, "West Scotland Area Meeting by telephone conference", in: *Scottish Friend*, February 2011, pp. 17–18.

Barton, David and Hamilton, Mary, *Local literacies: reading and writing in one community*. London: Routledge, 1998.

Burnell, Jan, *Taking and writing minutes*. London: Centre for Strategy and Communication, 2004.

Citizens Advice Bureau, *Writing minutes for trustee board meetings* (Bite Size Training), www.cablink.org.uk (last updated 14.12.10), visited 2.3.11.

Cronk, Sandra, *Gospel order* (Pendle Hill Pamphlet 297). Wallingford, PA: Pendle Hill, 1991.

Davis, Christine, *Minding the future* (Swarthmore Lecture). London: Quaker Books, 2008.

Duffy, Carol Ann, "White writing" in: *Feminine Gospels*. London: Picador, 2002; p. 57.

Eccles, Peter, *The presence in the midst* (Swarthmore Lecture). London: Quaker Books, 2009.

Fendall, Lon, Wood, Jan and Bishop, Bruce, *Practicing discernment together: finding God's way forward in decision making*. Newberg, OR: Barclay Press, 2007.

Frith, Judy, "The temporal collage: how British Quakers make choices about time", in *Quaker Studies* 15/1, 2010; pp. 53–66.

Bibliography

Gillman, Harvey, *A light that is shining*. London: Quaker Home Service, 2nd ed 2003.

Gutmann, Joanna, *Taking minutes of meetings*. London: Kogan Page, 2001.

Halliday, Robert, *Mind the oneness: the foundation of good Quaker business method*. London: Quaker Home Service, 1991; 2nd ed 2010.

Hammersley, Martyn, *What's wrong with ethnography?* London: Routledge, 1992.

Heathfield Margaret, *Being together* (Swarthmore lecture). London: Quaker Home Service, 1994.

Hoggart, Richard, *The uses of literacy*. Harmondsworth: Penguin Books, 1957.

Hoover, Sharon, "The task of the recording clerk: spiritual exercise and ministry", in *Friends Journal*, May 2011; pp. 18–20 and p. 35.

Kaal, Felicity, "The future of Quakerism in Britain Yearly Meeting", in *Friends Quarterly*, May 2010, pp. 64–85.

Kairos Palestine, *A moment of truth: a word of faith, hope and love from the heart of Palestinian suffering*. Distributed by Friends of Sabeel UK, 2009.

Krieger, Nancy, in: *Swiss Quaker life, belief and thought*, ed. Erica Royston and David Hay-Edie. Geneva: Switzerland Yearly Meeting of the Religious Society of Friends, 2009; p. 31.

Lacout, Pierre, *God is silence*, trans. John Kay. London: Quaker Home Service, 1993 (first published 1969).

Leonard, Alison, *Telling our stories: wrestling with a fresh language for the spiritual journey*. London: Darton, Longman and Todd, 1995.

Loring, Patricia, *Listening spirituality: vol II Corporate spiritual practice among Friends*. Washington DC: Openings Press, 1997.

Mace, Jane, *Working with words: literacy beyond school*. London: Chameleon Books with Writers and Readers Publishing Cooperative, 1979.

Mace, Jane, *Talking about literacy: principles and practice of adult literacy education*. London: Routledge, 1992.

Mace, Jane, "Signatures and the lettered world", in Crowther, Jim, Hamilton, Mary and Tett, Lyn (ed.), *Powerful literacies*. Leicester: NIACE, 2001; pp. 45–55.

Mace, Jane, *The give and take of writing: scribes, literacy and everyday life*. Leicester: NIACE, 2002.

Mace, Jane, "Silence and text in Quaker business meetings: notes from a research study", in: *RaPAL Journal*, vol. 76, spring/summer 2012, pp. 36–40.

Morley, Barry, *Beyond consensus: salvaging sense of the meeting* (Pendle Hill Pamphlet 307). Wallingford, PA: Pendle Hill, 1993.

Murgatroyd, Linda "The future of Quakers in Britain: holding spaces for the Spirit to act", in: *Friends Quarterly*, May 2010; pp. 4–48.

O'Shea, Ursula Jane, *Living the way: Quaker spirituality and community*. London: Quaker Books, 2003 (first published 1993).

Peters, Kate, *Print culture and the early Quakers*. Cambridge University Press, 2005.

Bibliography

Pink Dandelion, Ben, *The liturgies of Quakerism.* Aldershot: Ashgate Publishing, 2005.

Pink Dandelion, Ben, *The Quakers: a very short introduction.* Oxford University Press, 2008.

Pollard, Francis E., Pollard, Beatrice E. and Pollard, Robert S.W. *Democracy and the Quaker method.* London: Bannisdale Press, 1949.

Punshon, John, *Encounter with silence: reflections from the Quaker tradition.* Richmond, IN: Friends United Press, 1987.

Sharman, Cecil, *Servant of the meeting: Quaker business meetings and their clerks.* London: Quaker Home Service, 1983.

Sheeran, Michael J., *Beyond majority rule: voteless decisions in the Religious Society of Friends.* Philadelphia: Philadelphia Yearly Meeting of the Religious Society of Friends, 2nd ed. 1996.

Street, Brian V., *Literacy in theory and practice.* Cambridge University Press, 2001 (first published 1984).

Tusting, Karin, "The new literacy studies and time", in: Barton, David, Hamilton, Mary and Ivanic, Roz (ed.) *Situated literacies: reading and writing in context.* London: Routledge, 2000.

Vincent, David, *The rise of mass literacy: reading and writing in modern Europe.* Cambridge: Polity Press, 2000.

Wall, Ginny, *Deepening the life of the Spirit: resources for spiritual practice.* London: Quaker Books, 2012.

Wenger, Étienne, *Communities of practice: learning, meaning and identity.* Cambridge University Press, 1998.

Whitehouse, Derrick, *Towards an inspired Quaker meeting: the relevance and implementation of Gospel order* (the Workbook). Northampton: Whitehouse, 2009.